UK Price
£3.95

AN ILLUSTRATED GUIDE TO
GERMAN, ITALIAN AND JAPANESE
FIGHTERS
OF WORLD WAR II
Major Fighters and Attack Aircraft of the Axis Powers

AN ILLUSTRATED GUIDE TO
GERMAN, ITALIAN AND JAPANESE
FIGHTERS
OF WORLD WAR II
Major Fighters and Attack Aircraft of the Axis Powers

Bill Gunston

a Salamander book

Published by Salamander Books Limited
LONDON

A Salamander Book

© 1980 Salamander Books Ltd.,
Salamander House,
27 Old Gloucester Street,
London WC1N 3AF,
United Kingdom

ISBN 0 86101 064 7

Distributed in the United Kingdom by
New English Library Ltd.

Contents

Aircraft are arranged alphabetically by manufacturers' names, within
national groups.

Credits

Author: Bill Gunston, former
Technical Editor of *Flight
International*, Assistant Compiler of
Jane's All the World's Aircraft,
contributor to many Salamander
illustrated reference books.

Editor: Ray Bonds
Designer: Lloyd Martin

Colour and line drawings:
© Pilot Press Ltd.
Photographs: The publishers wish to
thank all the official international
governmental archives, aircraft and
systems manufacturers and private
collections who have supplied
photographs for this book.

Printed in Belgium by
Henri Proost et Cie.

GERMANY

Naturally, Nazi Germany planned carefully for every eventuality, and where possible had more than one type of aircraft for each combat mission as well as new designs coming along as the next generation. And if ever a fighter had an inauspicious start it was the Messerschmitt Bf 109, first flown at the end of May 1935. Not only was Messerschmitt himself extremely unpopular with top-ranking Nazis, including the air minister, but even impartial experts such as Ernst Udet, head of procurement and one of the world's most famous fighter pilots, said the new 109 would 'never make a fighter'. It was perhaps too advanced in concept, with a long rakish fuselage, shallow enclosed cockpit and amazingly small wing (though liberally endowed with slats and flaps). Yet the 109, instead of being laughed off the scene as many had expected, was not merely the fighter the Luftwaffe selected but it was virtually the only Luftwaffe fighter from 1937 until 1942. Production rose year by year to the final collapse in 1945, and when the last one was built (in Spain, actually, as late as 1958) the total handsomely exceeded 30,000, surpassing that of all other aircraft outside the Soviet Union.

This is all the more remarkable when it is recalled that the only other day fighter worth mentioning, the Fw 190, which flew shortly before the war and began to reach the squadrons in 1941, was in almost all respects superior. Though markedly heavier it was at least as compact, had an incredible capability of carrying guns, bombs and other weapons, and suffered from none of the shortcomings in handling that would have made the mass-produced Bf 109G – the standard 109 from 1942 onward – quite

unacceptable to any Allied air force. Yet while the 190 swiftly became the No 1 tactical multirole attack aircraft, the 109 stayed the No 1 fighter; and in the hands of someone used to its tricky and often unpleasant characteristics it was deadly. Most of the top-scoring Luftwaffe pilots, with 250 to 352 kills each, flew the 109 throughout their careers.

The Luftwaffe, however, also used two quite different species of fighter in World War II in a way paralleled only by Britain. One was the radar-equipped night fighter and the other the jet. Though some 109s and 190s achieved a few night kills the most successful aircraft for bringing down heavy night bombers were all large twins, notably the Bf 110 and Ju 88. The 110 had been intended as a day *zerstörer* (destroyer) to sweep defending fighters out of the path of the Luftwaffe's bombers, but the RAF demonstrated its inability to survive against modern single-seaters. The even larger Ju 88 was designed as a bomber, but in fact by 1944 it had become one of the world's greatest night interceptors with a selection of sensors to help it find its prey, and devastating armament, including cannon firing upwards into the bomber's defenceless undersides.

By late 1944 not only was the twin-jet Me 262 coming into service in numbers but the Luftwaffe also used the highly unconventional Me 163 rocket-propelled interceptor which made up in rate of climb what it lacked in range and endurance. Surprisingly, both were beautiful to fly once in the air, but they suffered from various other problems that restricted their value, and they were too late to stave off defeat.

Arado Ar 68

Ar 68G

Origin: Arado Handelsgesellschaft, Warnemünde.
Type: Single-seat fighter.
Engine: 750hp BMW VI 12-cylinder vee liquid-cooled.
Dimensions: Span 36ft 0in (11m); length 31ft 2in (9·5m); height 10ft 10in (3·3m).
Weights: Empty 3,307lb (1500kg); loaded 4,410lb (2000kg).
Performance: Maximum speed 192mph (310km/h) at 13,125ft (4000m); service ceiling 24,280ft (7400m); range with service load 342 miles (550km).
Armament: Two 7·92mm MG 17 machine guns above engine: racks for six 110lb (50kg) bombs.
History: First flight November 1933; (Ar 68G) December 1935; termination of production, probably 1937.

Development: Forbidden to have a warlike air force by the Versailles Treaty, Germany produced no combat aircraft in the 1920s and early 1930s, though German design teams did produce important prototypes in Spain, Sweden and Switzerland. By the time the Nazi party seized power in 1933 there was a useful nucleus of talent and industrial strength and the Arado firm was, with Heinkel, charged with urgently building a first-line fighter for the new Luftwaffe. The result was the Ar 68V1 prototype, powered by the trusty BMW VI engine, rated at 660hp and constructed of welded steel tube and wood, with fabric covering except over the forward and upper fuselage. Like all Arado aircraft of the period it had a tailplane well behind

Right: Probably the earliest colour scheme in this book is this Ar 68F-1, with upright V-12 BMW engine, serving with III/JG 135 at Bad Aibling in 1936-7. The Balkankreuz (Balkan cross) national marking of the period can be compared with the more familiar post-October 1939 type above.

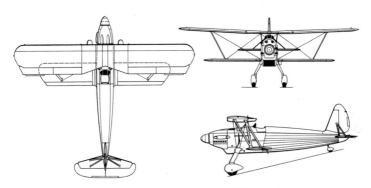

Above: Three-view of the Ar 68E with Jumo 210Da engine.

the fin and rudder, and the single-strut cantilever landing gear was distinctive. Two prototypes flew in 1934 with the 610hp Jumo 210 engine and this was selected for the production Ar 68E which entered service with the newly formed Luftwaffe in 1935. But the Ar 68F reverted to the BMW engine, uprated to 675hp, and the main production centred on the still more powerful Ar 68G. Despite good engines the Ar 68 was never an outstanding machine. It ran second in timing and performance to its great rival the He 51 and, apart from a few used as night fighters, had been relegated to training before World War II. One example of the Ar 68H, with BMW 132Dc radial and enclosed cockpit, was flown and a development, the Ar 197, would have been used aboard the carrier *Graf Zeppelin* had the vessel been commissioned.

Left: Typical of the many Arado 68 fighters and advanced trainers that survived into World War II, this Ar 68E-1 with Jumo 210Da engine served with a Jagdfliegerschule (fighter pilot school) in 1940. Spats were originally fitted to all three wheels, as in the three-view. Some Ar 68s served in 1940 as night fighters.

Arado Ar 234 Blitz

Ar 234B-1 and B-2 Blitz

Origin: Arado Flugzeugwerke GmbH.
Type: Single-seat reconnaissance (B-1) or attack bomber (B-2).
Engines: Two 1,980lb (900kg) thrust Junkers Jumo 004B axial turbojets.
Dimensions: Span 46ft 3½in (14·2m); length 41ft 5½in (12·65m); height 14ft 1¼in (4·3m).
Weights: Empty 11,464lb (5200kg); loaded 18,541lb (8410kg); maximum with rocket takeoff boost 21,715lb (9850kg).
Performance: Maximum speed (clean) 461mph (742km/h); service ceiling 32,800ft (10,000m); range (clean) 1,013 miles (1630km), (with 3,300lb bomb load) 684 miles (1100km).
Armament: Two fixed MG 151 20mm cannon in rear fuselage, firing to rear and sighted by periscope; various combinations of bombs slung under fuselage and/or engines to maximum of 3,300lb (1500kg).
History: First flight (Ar 234V1) 15 June 1943, (Ar 234V9 with landing gear) March 1944, (Ar 234B-0 pre-production) 8 June 1944; operational delivery September 1944.
User: Germany (Luftwaffe).

Development: As the first jet reconnaissance bomber, the Ar 234 Blitz (meaning Lightning) spearheaded Germany's remarkably bold introduction of high-performance turbojet aircraft in 1944. Its design was begun under Walter Blume in 1941, after long studies in 1940 of an official specification for a jet-propelled reconnaissance aircraft with a range of 1,340 miles. The design was neat and simple, with two of the new axial engines slung under a high wing, and the single occupant in a pressurised cockpit forming the entire nose. But to achieve the required fuel capacity no wheels were fitted. When it flew on 15 June 1943 the first 234 took off from a three-wheel trolley and landed on retractable skids. After extensive trials with eight prototypes the ninth flew with conventional landing gear, leading through 20 pre-production models to the operational 234B-1, with ejection seat, autopilot and drop tanks under the engines. Main production centred on the 234B-2, made in many sub-variants, most of them able to carry a heavy bomb load. Service over the British Isles with the B-1 began in September 1944, followed by a growing force of B-2s which supported the Battle of the Bulge in the winter 1944–45. In March 1945 B-2s of III/KG76 repeatedly attacked the vital Remagen bridge across the Rhine with 2,205lb (1,000kg) bombs, causing its collapse. Though handicapped by fuel shortage these uninterceptable aircraft played a significant role on all European fronts in the closing months of the war, 210 being handed over excluding the many prototypes and later versions with four engines and an uncompleted example with a crescent-shaped wing.

Below: The Ar 234 was the only jet bomber to be operational in World War II, and though it did not affect the course of the war its pinpricks were usually unstoppable. This B-2/P Blitz served with 9/KG 76 operating from Achmer in February 1945. It is seen with 1,102-lb (SC500) bombs hung under the nacelles.

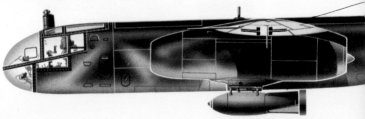

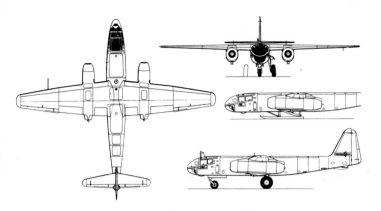

Above: Three-view of Ar 234B-2 (inset, Ar 234 V1 prototype).

Above: First takeoff by the Ar 234 V9 (ninth prototype) at Alt Lönnewitz on 10 March 1944, with 66 Imp gal drop tanks. This was the first of the B-series, with landing gear; it also introduced pressurization and an ejection seat, one of the first on any production aircraft. This photograph was a frame from a ciné film in which it could be seen that the pale colour in the right jet nozzle was a sudden gout of flame!

Arado Ar240

Ar prototypes ABC series and 440

Origin: Arado Flugzeugwerke GmbH.
Type: Zerstörer, heavy fighter, see text.
Engines: Two Daimler-Benz inverted-vee-12 liquid-cooled, see text.
Dimensions: Span (A-0) 43ft 9in (13·33m), (C-0) 54ft 5in (16·59m); length (A-0) 42ft 0¼in (12·81m); height 12ft 11½in (3·95m).
Weights: Empty (A-0) 13,669lb (6200kg), (C-0) 18,650lb (8460kg); maximum (A-0) 22,700lb (10,297kg), (C-0) 25,850lb (11,726kg).
Performance: Maximum speed (A-0) 384mph (618km/h), (C-0) 454mph (730km/h) with GM-1 boost at high alt.; max range (A-0) 1,242 miles (2000km).
Armament: (A-0) two fixed 7·92mm MG 17 and two remote-control barbettes each with two 7·92mm MG 81; (C-0) four fixed 20mm MG 151 and two barbettes each with two 13mm MG 131, plus external bomb load up to 3,968lb (1800kg).
History: First flight (V1) 10 May 1940, (A-0) October 1942, (C-0) March 1943, (440) early summer 1942.

Development: In 1938 Arado's technical director, Walter Blume, began studies which were intended to lead to an outstandingly advanced and formidable multi-role combat aircraft, but instead led to years of effort with little reward. Features of the E240 study included tandem seats in a pres-surized cockpit, high-lift slats and flaps on a highly loaded wing, a unique

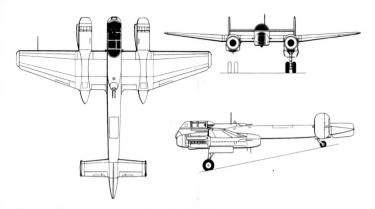

Above: Three-view of the Ar 240A-01 with ducted spinners.

dive brake doubling as the tailcone, and upper and lower rear gun barbettes sighted by the observer through an upper/lower magnifying periscope system. But from the start the Ar 240 was dogged by technical misfortune, the enduring problem being unacceptable flying characteristics (the V1 prototype was unstable about all three axes). Later aircraft switched from the 1,075hp DB 601 to the 1,750hp DB 603A, 1,475hp DB 605AM, 1,900hp DB 603G or BMW 801TJ radial.

Below: The Ar 240 V3 of spring 1941, with conventional spinners.

Bachem Ba 349 Natter

Ba 349 V1-V16, A and B series

Origin: Bachem-Werke GmbH, Waldsee.
Type: Part-expendable target-defence interceptor.
Engine: 4,410lb (2000kg) thrust Walter HWK 109-509C-1 bi-propellant rocket (vertical launch boosted by four 1,102lb (500kg) or two 2,205lb (1000kg) solid motors).
Dimensions: Span 11ft 9¾in (3·6m); length (A) 19ft 9in (6·02m); height (flying attitude) 7ft 4½in (2·25m).
Weights: Empty 1,940lb (880kg); loaded (with boost rockets) 4,920lb (2232kg).
Performance: Maximum speed (sea level) 497mph (800km/h), (at high altitude) 621mph (1000km/h); rate of climb 36,417ft (11,100m)/min; range after climb 20–30 miles (32–48km).
Armament: 24 Föhn 73mm spin-stabilized rockets, or 33 R4M 55mm spin-stabilized rockets, or (proposed) two 30mm MK 108 cannon each with 30 rounds.

Development: One of the most radical and desperate "fighters" ever built, the Natter (Viper) was born of necessity. In the summer of 1944 the mounting weight of daylight attacks by the US 8th Air Force called for unconventional defences, and the Luftwaffe picked a proposal by Dipl-Ing Erich Bachem for a manned interceptor which could be stationed in the path of hostile heavy bombers. As the American formations passed overhead the interceptor would be blasted vertically off the ground, thereafter climbing almost vertically on an internal rocket. Nearing the bombers, the pilot would sight on one and fire his battery of missiles. He would then use his remaining kinetic energy to climb higher than the bombers and swoop back for a ramming attack. Just before impact he was to trigger a mechanism to separate his seat (or front fuselage) and the rear portion with rocket motor.

Tests showed that no simple ejection system could be incorporated, and

Below: One of the Ba 349A Natters, armed with 24 Hs 217 Föhn (Storm) rockets exposed with the streamlined nosecap removed. The interceptor is strapped to its cradle on which it was then to be transported to the launch gantry on a special trailer for elevation to about 87°.

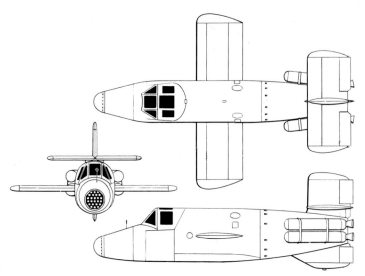

Above: Three-view of the Ba 349B (production aircraft).

the essence of the Natter was simplicity. The structure was wood, apart from the simple metal body with armoured cockpit. Eventually the ramming attack was abandoned, and the only parts saved were the pilot and rocket motor, for hopeful re-use. Following pilotless tests from the near-vertical ramp, and piloted gliding trials towed by an He 111 to about 18,000ft, the first manned shot was attempted on 28 February 1945. At about five seconds from lift-off the canopy came away (apparently hitting Oberleutnant Lothar Siebert) and the Natter curved over and crashed. By April 36 had flown, seven with pilots, but Allied troops overran the factory and launch site before any combat missions could take place.

Below: This almost complete Ba 349A was discovered by Allied troops in May 1945 strapped to its cradle and mounted on its towing trailer. The canopy is unlatched, and the jettisonable plastic nosecap is not fitted. On another trailer is one of the Schmidding solid-fuel takeoff rockets.

Blohm und Voss BV40

Bv40 V1 to V19 and BV 40A

Origin: Blohm und Voss (Abt. Flugzeugbau).
Type: Point-defence interceptor glider.
Dimensions: Span 25ft 11in (7·90m); length 18ft 8½in (5·70m); height 5ft 4¼in (1·66m).
Weights: Empty 1,844lb (836kg); maximum 2,094lb (950kg).
Performance: Maximum speed (Bf 109G tug) 344mph (553km/h), (109G towing two BV 40s) 315mph (507km/h); anticipated diving speed in free flight 560mph (900km/h); time to climb to 23,000ft (7000m), (one BV 40) 12 min, (two BV 40s) 16·8min.
Armament: Two 30mm MK 108 each with 35 rounds.
History: First flight, late May 1944.

Development: Desperate situations lead to desperate remedies, and often to genuine technical progress. This was certainly the case in the Luftwaffe's attempts to inflict heavier losses on the US 8th Air Force daylight bomber formations. One answer was the Ba 349, and an even stranger one was a glider, proposed by BV's technical director Richard Vogt. The reasoning was simple: the only way to reduce the chances of fighters being hit by the hail of fire from a B-17 formation was to reduce the frontal area, and the best way to do this was to eliminate the engine. Moreover, most of the BV 40 was planned for simple and cheap production on a vast scale by woodworkers, while the metal cockpit was to be protected by armour and thick glass representing more than one-quarter of the gross weight. Vogt hoped to use

Blohm und Voss BV155

Me 155A and B, Bv 155 V1 to V3

Origin: Messerschmitt AG, later Blohm und Voss, Abt. Flugzeugbau.
Type: High-altitude interceptor.
Engine: (155B) DB 603A with TKL 15 turbocharger giving 1,450hp at 49,210ft (15,000m).
Dimensions: Span (B) 67ft 3in (20·5m); length 39ft 4½in (12·00m); height 9ft 9½in (2·98m).
Weights: (B) empty 10,734lb (4870kg); loaded (max armament) 13,263lb (6016kg).
Performance: (B) maximum speed 429mph (690km/h) at 52,493ft (16,000m); range at high alt, about 895 miles (1440km).

Development: Messerschmitt began the Me 155 as a derivative of the Bf 109 to operate from the resumed carrier *Graf Zeppelin*, but when this unhappy ship again fell from favour the 155 reappeared as a pinpoint bomber with 2,205lb (1000kg) bomb and finally in 1943 as a long-span interceptor to hit high-flying US bombers. In August 1943 work was passed from Messerschmitt (said to be overloaded) to Blohm und Voss, but the two firms disagreed violently on the design. The whole job eventually became the Bv 155, but had to be redesigned. The Bv 155 V1 flew on 1 September 1944 and a further redesign, the V2, in February 1945. With outstanding propulsion and aerodynamic features they would have been unmatched by Allied fighters at heights over 40,000ft, and were intended to have heavy groups of 15, 20 or 30mm cannon. At the final collapse work was well advanced on the V4 (C-series) with fuselage radiators.

Right: The BV 155 V3, still unfinished, at Farnborough in late 1945.

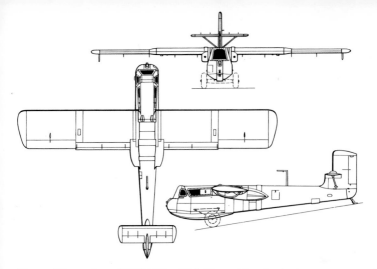

Above: Three-view of BV 40 V1, with jettisonable wheels shown.

one 30mm cannon and trail an explosive charge on a long wire for a second attacking pass, but the best answer was found to be two heavy guns to pump out the maximum firepower in the brief period available in a head-on attack. The whole programme was abandoned in the autumn of 1944 when the flight-test phase had been completed, with six of 19 prototypes, and studies were in hand for heavy bomb loads for release above bomber formations.

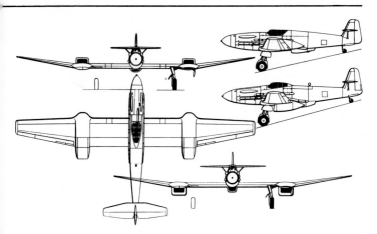

Above: Three-view of BV 155 V2 and V3 with (above) two views of V1.

Dornier Do 335 Pfeil

Do 335A-1 and A-6

Origin: Dornier-Werke GmbH.
Type: (A-1) single-seat fighter, (A-6) two-seat night fighter.
Engines: Two 1,900hp Daimler-Benz DB 603G 12-cylinder inverted-vee liquid-cooled, in push/pull arrangement.
Dimensions: Span 45ft 4in (13·8m); length 45ft 6in (13·87m); height 16ft 4in (4m).
Weights: Empty (A-1) 16,314lb (7400kg); (A-6) 16,975lb (7700kg); maximum loaded (both) 25,800lb (11,700kg).
Performance: Maximum speed (A-1) 413mph (665km/h) sustained; 477mph (765km/h) emergency boost (A-6 about 40mph slower in each case); initial climb (A-1) 4,600ft (1400m)/min; service ceiling (A-1) 37,400ft (11,410m); (A-6) 33,400ft (10,190m); maximum range (both) 1,280 miles (2050km) clean, up to 2,330 miles (3750km) with drop tank.
Armament: Typical A-1, one 30mm MK 103 cannon firing through front propeller hub and two 15mm MG 151/15 above nose; underwing racks for light stores and centreline rack for 1,100lb (500kg) bomb; A-6 did not carry bomb and usually had 15mm guns replaced by 20mm MG 151/20s.
History: First flight (Do 335V1) autumn 1943; (production A-1) late November 1944.
User: Germany (Luftwaffe).

Development: Dornier took out a patent in 1937 for an aircraft powered by two engines, one behind the other, in the fuselage, driving tractor and pusher propellers. In 1939–40 Schempp-Hirth built the Gö 9 research aircraft to test the concept of a rear propeller driven by an extension shaft and in 1941 work began on the Do 231 fighter-bomber. This was replaced by the Do 335 and by first flight Dornier had orders for 14 prototypes, ten preproduction A-0s, 11 production A-1s and three dual-control trainer A-10 and A-12 with stepped tandem cockpits. At high speed the 335 was prone to unpleasant porpoising and snaking, but production continued on the A-1, the A-4 reconnaissance batch and the A-6 with FuG 220 radar

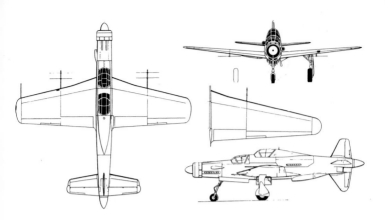

Above: Three-view of the Do 335A-6 two-seat night fighter with (inset) the long-span wing of B-8.

operated by a rear-seat observer. Though heavy, the 335 was strong and very fast and was notable in having the first production type of ejection seat (for obvious reasons). By VE-day about 90 aircraft had been rolled out, more than 60 flown and about 20 delivered to combat units. Work was also well advanced on a number of versions of the Do 335B heavy fighter, with added 30mm MK 108 cannon in the wings (some having two-stage engines and long-span wings), the Do 435 with various very powerful engines, and the twinned Do 635 with two Do 335 fuselages linked by a new parallel centre-section. The 635, which was being designed and produced by Junkers as the 8-635, would have weighed 72,000lb as a reconnaissance aircraft, and flown 4,050 miles cruising at 398mph. Pfeil means "arrow"

Below: The Do 335 V1 (first prototype), which flew on 26 October 1943. Pilots were enthusiastic, and 348mph (560km/h) was recorded with the front propeller feathered.

Focke-Wulf Fw 187 Falke

Fw 187 V1 to V6 and A0

Origin: Focke-Wulf Flugzeugbau GmbH.
Type: Zerstörer, heavy fighter.
Engines: Two Junkers Jumo 210 inverted-vee-12 liquid-cooled, (V1) 680hp 210Da, (most) 730hp 210Ga, (V6) 1,000hp DB 600A.
Dimensions: Span 50ft 2½in (15·30m); length 36ft 5½in (11·01m); height 12ft 7in (3·85m).
Weights: Empty (A-0) 8,157lb (3700kg); maximum 11,023lb (5000kg).
Performance: (A-0) Maximum speed 326mph (525km/h); initial climb, 3,445ft (1050m)/min; service ceiling 32,800ft (10,000m).
Armament: Four 7·92mm MG 17 and two 20mm MG FF.
History: First flight, early May 1937, (A-0) about February 1939.

Development: Though for various reasons it never went into production, Focke-Wulf's Fw 187 Falke (Falcon) was an extremely fine basis for development and, according to all accounts, could have led to an outstanding family of multi-role aircraft. The cramped single-seat V1 prototype was 50mph (80km/h) faster than the contemporary Bf 109B with two similar engines, despite the fact it weighed more than twice as much and had roughly double the range. The V3 was the first with a more spacious

Right: One of the 1940 propaganda photographs showing Fw 187A-0 zerstörers of the so-called Werkschutzstaffel Bremen, which was one of a number of locally raised units maintained and flown by manufacturer's personnel to defend aircraft factories. Only three such aircraft existed, but Goebbels' propaganda machine issued a stream of pictures to give the impression this was the Luftwaffe's new zerstörer (destroyer, ie heavy fighter).

Below: 'Zerstörer number 7' in the pseudo Luftwaffe long-range fighter staffel.

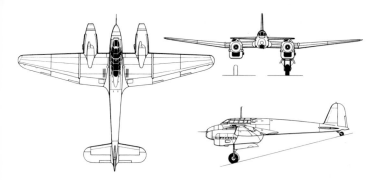

Above: Three-view of the Fw 187A-0.

tandem-seat cockpit, alongside which were the four MG 17s, the cannon being under the floor. The V6 reached 392mph (631km/h) on two DB 600A engines, faster than any other fighter in January 1939. Official interest in this promising fighter was slight, and only three A-0 pre-production Falkes were built, being used in combat by an Industrie-Schutzstaffel defending the company works at Bremen (Dipl-Ing Mehlhorn allegedly scored several kills). In the winter 1940–41 the trio were loaned to a Jagdstaffel in Norway, where they were said to be much preferred to the Bf 110; but when the RLM heard about it they were immediately recalled.

Focke-Wulf Fw 189 Uhu

Fw 189A-1, -2 and -3

Origin: Focke-Wulf Flugzeugbau GmbH; built under Focke-Wulf control by SNCASO, with outer wings from Breguet.

Type: Three-seat reconnaissance and close support.

Engines: Two 465hp Argus As 410A-1 12 cylinder inverted-vee air-cooled.

Dimensions: Span 60ft 4½in (18·4m); length 39ft 4½in (12m); height 10ft 2in (3·1m).

Weights: Empty 5,930lb (2690kg); loaded 8,708lb (3950kg).

Performance: Maximum speed 217mph (350km/h); climb to 13,120ft (4000m) in 8 min 20sec; service ceiling 23,950ft (7300m); range 416 miles (670km).

Armament: (A-2) one 7·92mm MG17 machine gun in each wing root, twin 7·92mm MG81 manually aimed in dorsal position and (usually) twin MG 81 in rear cone with limited field of fire; underwing racks for four 110lb (50kg) bombs.

History: First flight (Fw 189V1) July 1938; first delivery (pre-production Fw 189A-0) September 1940; final delivery August 1944.

User: Germany (Luftwaffe), Hungary, Slovakia.

Development: Today the diversity of aircraft layout makes us forget how odd this aircraft seemed. It looked strange to the customer also, but after outstandingly successful flight trials the 189 Uhu (Owl) was grudgingly bought in quantity as a standard reconnaissance aircraft. Though it flew in numbers well before the war — no two prototypes being alike — it was unknown by the Allies until it was disclosed in 1941 as "the Flying Eye" of the German armies. On the Eastern front it performed beyond all expectation, for it retained its superb handling (which made it far from a sitting duck to fighters) and also showed great toughness of structure and more than once returned to base with one tail shot off or removed by Soviet ramming attack. Attempts to produce special attack versions with small heavily armoured nacelles were not so successful, but 10 Fw 189B trainers were built with a conventional nacelle having side-by-side dual controls in a normal cockpit, with an observer above the trailing edge. The Fw 189A-3 was another dual-control version having the normal "glasshouse". Eventually the sole source became French factories with assembly at Bordeaux-Mérignac (today the Dassault Mirage plant), which halted as Allied armies approached. There were many different versions and several developments with more powerful engines, but the basic A-1, A-2 (better armament) and A-3 were the only types built in numbers, the total of these versions being 846.

Below: Though most Fw 189s served in the reconnaissance role this tough and manoeuvrable bird also flew close-support missions and with FuG 212 Lichtenstein C1 radar served as a night fighter. This particular machine, an A-1, served with 1(H)/32 at Petsamo (northern Finland) in December 1942.

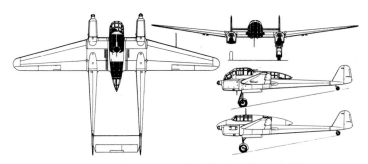

Above: Three-view of Fw 189A-2, with side view (lower) of B-0.

Below: Luftwaffe ground-recon trooper with an A-1 in USSR.

Focke-Wulf Fw 190 and Ta 152

Fw 190A series, D series, F series, G series and Ta 152

Origin: Focke-Wulf Flugzeugbau GmbH; extremely dispersed manufacture and assembly, and part-subcontracted to Brandt (SNCA du Centre), France; also built in France post-war.

Type: Single-seat fighter bomber.

Engine: (A-8, F-8) one 1,700hp (2,100hp emergency boost) BMW 801Dg 18-cylinder two-row radial; (D-9) one 1,776hp (2,240hp emergency boost) Junkers Jumo 213A-1 12-cylinder inverted-vee liquid-cooled; (Ta 152H-1) one 1,880hp (2,250hp) Jumo 213E-1.

Dimensions: Span 34ft $5\frac{1}{2}$in (10·49m); (Ta 152H-1) 47ft $6\frac{3}{4}$in (14·5m); length (A-8, F-8) 29ft 0in (8·84m); (D-9) 33ft $5\frac{1}{4}$in (10·2m); (Ta 152H-1) 35ft $5\frac{1}{2}$in (10·8m); height 13ft 0in (3·96m); (D-9) 11ft $0\frac{1}{2}$in (3·35m); (Ta 152H-1) 11ft 8in (3·55m).

Weights: Empty (A-8, F-8) 7,055lb (3200kg); (D-9) 7,720lb (3500kg); (Ta 152H-1) 7,940lb (3600kg); loaded (A-8, F-8) 10,800lb (4900kg); (D-9) 10,670lb (4840kg); (Ta 152H-1) 12,125lb (5500kg).

Performance: Maximum speed (with boost) (A-8, F-8) 408mph (653km/h); (D-9) 440mph (704km/h); (Ta 152H-1) 472mph (755km/h); initial climb (A-8, F-8) 2,350ft (720m)/min; (D-9, Ta 152) about 3,300ft (1000m)/min; service ceiling (A-8, F-8) 37,400ft (11,410m); (D-9) 32,810ft (10,000m); (Ta 152H-1) 49,215ft (15,000m); range on internal fuel (A-8, F-8 and D-9) about 560 miles (900km); (Ta 152H-1), 745 miles (1200km).

Armament: (A-8, F-8) two 13mm MG 131 above engine, two 20mm MG 151/20 in wing roots and two MG 151/20 or 30mm MK 108 in outer wings; (D-9) as above, or without outer MG 151/20s, with provision for 30mm MK 108 firing through propeller hub; (Ta 152H-1) one 30mm

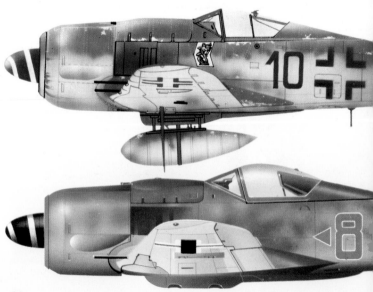

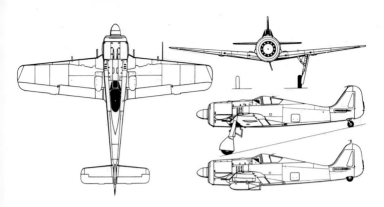

Above: Three-view of Fw 190A-3 with side view of A-4/U1.

MK 108 and two inboard MG 151/20 (sometimes outboard MG 151/20s as well); bomb load (A-8, D-9) one 1,100lb (500kg) on centreline; (F-8) one 3,968lb (1800kg) on centreline; (Ta 152H-1) (some reconnaissance H-models unarmed).
History: First flight (Fw 190V1) June 1, 1939, (production Fw 190A-1) September 1940, (Fw 190D) late 1942.
Users: Croatia, Germany (Luftwaffe), Slovakia, Turkey; post-war, Argentina, France (Armée de l'Air, Aéronavale).

Development: Though flown well before World War II this trim little fighter was unknown to the Allies and caused a nasty surprise when first met over France in early 1941. Indeed, it was so far superior to the bigger and more sluggish Spitfire V that for the first time the RAF felt not only outnumbered but beaten technically. In June 1942 an Fw 190A-3 landed by mistake in England, and the Focke-Wulf was discovered to be even better than expected. It was faster than any Allied fighter in service, had far heavier armament (at that time the standard was two 7·92mm MG 17s over ▶

Left: Built in greater numbers than any other version, the Fw 190A-8 was a versatile fighter and attack aircraft. It retained the MG 131 fuselage guns of the A-7, which caused the bulge ahead of the windscreen, and had the powerful armament of four MG 151 cannon in the wings. MW50 boosting was added to the engine. The aircraft shown served II/JG 11 at Darmstadt in early 1945, with yellow 'Eastern Front' theatre band.

Left: This F-8, serving with SG 4 at Köln-Wahn in December 1944, is typical of the chief family of close-support versions of the Fw 190 which from 1943 gradually equipped virtually all the Schlachtgruppen supporting the German ground forces. Most F-series had a belly rack for a 1,102-lb bomb, plus wing racks (not fitted here) for two 551lb. Note the bulged canopy.

the engine, two of the previously unknown Mauser cannon inboard and two 20mm MG FF outboard), was immensely strong, had excellent power of manoeuvre and good pilot view. It was also an extremely small target, much lighter than any Allied fighter and had a stable widetrack landing gear (unlike the Bf 109). Altogether it gave Allied pilots and designers an inferiority complex. Though it never supplanted the 109, it was subsequently made in a profusion of different versions by many factories.

The A series included many fighter and fighter bomber versions, some having not only the increasingly heavy internal armament but also two or four 20mm cannon or two 30mm in underwing fairings. Most had an emergency power boost system, using MW 50 (methanol/water) or GM-1 (nitrous oxide) injection, or both. Some carried torpedoes, others were two-seaters, and a few had autopilots for bad weather and night interceptions. The F series were close-support attack aircraft, some having the Panzerblitz array of R4M rockets for tank-busting (also lethal against heavy bombers). There were over 40 other special armaments, and some versions had armoured leading edges for ramming Allied bombers. The G was another important series of multi-role fighter/dive bombers, but by 1943 the main effort was devoted to what the RAF called the "long-nosed 190", the 190D. This went into production in the autumn of 1944, after much development, as the Fw 190D-9 ("Dora 9"). This was once more the fastest fighter in the sky and the later D-models were redesignated Ta 152 in honour of the director of Focke-Wulf's design team, Dipl Ing Kurt Tank. The early 152C ▶

Below: Fw 190G-3 long-range attack models over Romania in 1944.

Above: A row of Fw 190A-4 fighters with pilots at cockpit readiness, on a French airfield in 1943. This mottled camouflage was unusual on fighter 190s at this time, though it was seen on Jabo 190s bombing English coasts.

Below: This Fw 190A-5/U13 has been modified to F-8 standard with MG 131 fuselage guns and racks for a 1,102lb and two 551lb bombs.

Below: The very heavily armed Ta 152C-0/R11 (Ta 152C V7).

Above: Swinging the compass of the fifth Ta 152H at Cottbus.

series were outstandingly formidable, but the long-span H sacrificed guns for speed and height. Tank himself easily outpaced a flight of P-51 Mustangs which surprised him on a test flight; but only ten of the H sub-type had flown when the war ended. Altogether 20,051 Fw 190s were delivered, plus a small number of Ta 152s (67, excluding development aircraft). It is curious that the Bf 109, a much older and less attractive design with many shortcomings, should have been made in greater quantity and flown by nearly all the Luftwaffe's aces.

In 1945 the Fw 190A-5 was put into production at an underground plant in France managed by SNCASO. By 1946 a total of 64 had been delivered.

Focke-Wulf Ta 154

Ta 154 V1 to V15 and C series

Origin: Focke-Wulf Flugzeugbau GmbH, prototypes to V7 at Hanover—Langenhagen, V8—V15 (A-0 series) at Erfurt, production A-1 at Posen, Poland.
Type: Night and all-weather fighter.
Engines: Two Junkers Jumo inverted-vee-12 liquid-cooled, (V1, 2) 1,520hp 211N, (V3-V15, A-1) 1,750hp 213E, (C) 1,776hp 213A.
Dimensions: Span 52ft 6in (16·00m); length (with SN-2) 41ft 2¾in (12·56m); height (most) 11ft 9¾in (3·60m).
Weights: (A-1) Empty 14,122lb (6405kg); max loaded 21,050lb (9548kg).
Performance: Maximum speed (A-1) 404mph (650km/h); service ceiling 35,760ft (10,900m); range (two drop tanks) 1,156 miles (1850km).
Armament: (A-0, A-1) two 30mm MK 108 and two 20mm MG 151 in sides of fuselage.

Development: Hailed by the propaganda machine as "Germany's Mosquito", the wooden Ta 154 had an excellent performance and came near to being a major combat type. The Luftwaffe never considered defensive aircraft at all until 1941; then, for obvious reasons, in September 1942 the RLM issued a specification for a fighter to shoot down RAF heavy bombers at night. Tank had the Ta 154 V1 flying by 7 July 1943, and development generally went well, though the whole project posed inherently high risk in the use of wood for the structure of so advanced an aircraft. It was only the need to conserve light alloy, and the great success of the British Mosquito, that drove this policy relentlessly forward. By the summer of 1944 all 15 development aircraft had flown, most with C-1 or later SN-2 Lichtenstein radar, and A-1 production machines were coming off the line in Poland. The 154C was to follow, with two ejection seats under a sliding bubble canopy and Schräge Musik 30mm cannon, while the Ta 254 was a still later family. But on 28 June 1944 the second A-1 broke up in flight. It was found that, whereas the Tego-Film bonding used in earlier aircraft was satisfactory, the cold glue hastily brought in as adhesive after destruction

Above: Although described by Focke-Wulf as an Fw 190A-1, this is in fact a late A-0 fitted with MG FF outboard cannon like an A-1. This was the very first production version, in 1940.

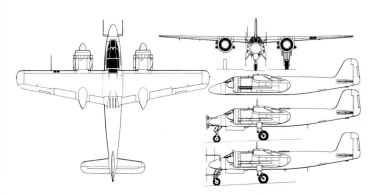

Above: Ta 154 V15, with side view of V1 (top) and V3 (centre).

by the RAF of the Tego-Film plant contained excess acid which ate away the wood. The 154 thus never got into service — not even six Pulk-Zerstörer conversions packed with explosives intended to break up US bomber formations.

Below: Third prototype, with Jumo 213s, radar and full armament.

Heinkel He 51

He 51A-1, B-2 and C-1

Origin: Ernst Heinkel AG; production see text.
Type: Single-seat fighter (B-2) reconnaissance seaplane; (C-1) land ground attack.
Engine: One 750hp BMW VI 7·3Z vee-12 water-cooled.
Dimensions: Span 36ft 1in (11m); length 27ft 6⅔in (8·4m); (B-2) about 31ft; height 10ft 6in (3·2m); (B-2) about 11ft.
Weights: (A-1), empty 3,223lb (1462kg); loaded 4,189lb (1900kg).
Performance: Maximum speed (A-1) 205mph (330km/h); initial climb 1,969ft (600m)/min; service ceiling 24,610ft (7500m); range 242 miles (390km).
Armament: Standard, two 7·92mm Rheinmetall MG 17 synchronised above fuselage; (B-2) same plus underwing racks for up to six 22lb (10kg) bombs; (C-1) same plus underwing racks for four 110lb (50kg) bombs.
History: First flight (He 49a) November 1932; (He 49b) February 1933; (He 51A-0) May 1933; service delivery of A-1, July 1934.
Users: Germany, Spain.
Development: Gradually, as the likelihood of Allied legal action receded, Heinkel dared to build aircraft that openly contravened the Versailles Treaty. The most startling was the He 37, obviously a prototype fighter, which in 1928 achieved 194mph, or 20mph faster than the RAF Bulldog which was still a year away from service. Land and seaplane versions led to a succession of He 49 fighter prototypes in the 1930s and these in turn provided the basis for the refined He 51. After the Ar 65 this was the first fighter ordered into production by the Reichsluftfahrtministerium for the reborn Luftwaffe. Though the initial order for He 51A-1s was only 75, Heinkel was unused to such an order and many were built under licence by Ago, Erla, Arado and Fieseler — which were also fast tooling for their own designs. In March 1935 the Luftwaffe was publicly announced, and JG1 "Richthofen" fighter squadron was combat-ready at Döberitz with its new Heinkels. In November 1936, 36 He 51A-1s went to Spain with the Legion Kondor, giving a sufficiently good showing for the Nationalists to buy at least 30 from Heinkel. There followed a total of 50 of various He 51B seaplane versions, the 38 B-2s being for service aboard cruisers. The final batch comprised 79 C-1 ground attack fighters, of which 28 served in Spain. The He 51 was still in active service in September 1939, operating in the close-support role in Poland, and remained as an advanced trainer until 1943.

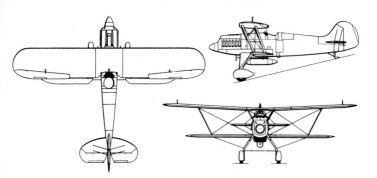

Above: Three-view of He 51C-1 (the B-1 was very similar).

Above: One of the surviving He 51B-1s photographed in about 1941 when it was serving as an advanced trainer at an A/B Schule, with drop tank to increase utilization. Guns were often fitted.

Left: After the start of World War II no He 51s were left in the front-line fighter role, though large numbers continued as advanced trainers and in utility roles. Most were assigned to the A/B schulen (pilot schools) or Jagdfliegerschulen (fighter-pilot schools) which were located all over German-occupied Europe. This He 51B was on the strength of A/B 123 at Agram (Zagreb, Yugoslavia) in the spring of 1942. By this time the spats over the main wheels had almost always been removed, though it was retained on the tailwheel. Colourful badges and emblems continued to be worn even in the training role, and often (as in this case) a theatre band was worn round the rear fuselage.

Heinkel He 100

He 100 V1 to V8 and 100D-1

Origin: Ernst Heinkel AG.
Type: Single-seat fighter.
Engine: 1,175hp Daimler-Benz DB 601 Aa inverted-vee-12 liquid-cooled.
Dimensions: Span 30ft 10¾in (9·41m); length 26ft 10¾in (8·195m); height 11ft 9¾in (3·60m).
Weights: (D-1) empty 3,990lb (1810kg); max loaded 5,512lb (2500kg).
Performance: (D-1) maximum speed 416mph (670km/h); service ceiling 36,090ft (11,000m); range 559 miles (900km).

Development: Undaunted by loss of the Luftwaffe's fighter orders to BFW with the 109, Heinkel proposed a much faster fighter, with structure completely different from the rather unimpressive He 112 to make it more efficient and much quicker and cheaper to build. The resulting Projekt 1035 was completed on 25 May 1937 and at the end of that year the now-informed RLM sanctioned a prototype and ten pre-production machines. Heinkel managed to secure the number "100" though this had been previously alotted to Fieseler. The first prototype flew on 22 January 1938, and was clearly outstandingly fast, being small and having a surface-evaporation cooling system instead of a draggy radiator. Though there were many problems, and Luftwaffe test pilots disliked the high wing loading, Udet himself flew the V2 to a new world 100km circuit record at 394·6mph (634·73km/h). On 30 March 1939 Hans Dieterle, flying the clipped-wing V3, took the world speed record at 463·92mph (746·6km/h). But the RLM saw no reason for mass production, and six prototypes were sold to the Soviet Union and three He 100D-0 to Japan, with armament of two MG 17

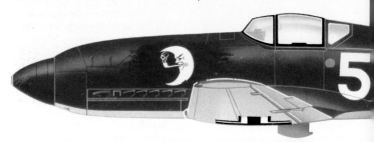

Below: One of the many photographs put out by the propaganda minister, Josef Goebbels, showing the 'He 113' in Luftwaffe use.

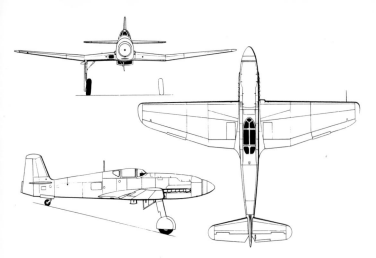

Above: Three-view of the Heinkel He 100D-1c.

and a 20mm MG/FF. The remaining 12 He 100D-1 fighters formed a Heinkel-Rostock defence unit, but in 1940 were publicised by Goebbels' propaganda machine in such a way as to convince Britain there was a fighter in large-scale service called the "He 113".

Left: Appearance of one of the dozen He 100D-1c pre-production fighters after it had been painted in completely fictitious 'unit markings' in 1940 for many widely published photographs describing the type as the non-existent 'He 113'. Of course, RAF pilots in late 1940 reported meeting He 113s over Germany! For sheer speed the He 100 had no rival in its day.

Below: This was one of the photographs issued to try to convince people the 'He 113' was a night fighter. Same aircraft shown above.

Heinkel He 112

He 112B-0 and B-1

Origin: Ernst Heinkel AG.
Type: Single-seat fighter and light ground attack.
Engine: One 680hp Junkers Jumo 210Ea inverted-vee-12 liquid-cooled.
Dimensions: (He 112) span 29ft 10$\frac{1}{4}$in (9·1m); length 30ft 6in (9·3m); height 12ft 7$\frac{1}{2}$in (3·85m).
Weights: Empty 3,571lb (1620kg); loaded 4,960lb (2250kg).
Performance: Maximum speed 317mph (510km/h); initial climb 2,300ft (700m)/min; service ceiling 27,890ft (8500m); range 684 miles (1100km).
Armament: Two 20mm Oerlikon MG FF cannon in outer wings and two 7·92mm Rheinmetall MG 17 machine guns in sides of fuselage; underwing racks for six 22lb (10kg) fragmentation bombs.
History: First flight (He 112V-1) September 1935; (B-series production prototype) May 1937; final delivery (Romania) September 1939.

Development: One of the first requirements issued by the rapidly expanded RLM under the Nazis was a specification for a completely new monoplane fighter to replace the Ar 68 and He 51. Heinkel's team under the Gunthers used He 70 experience to create the shapely He 112, which was much smaller and of wholly light-alloy stressed skin construction. Powered by a British Kestrel, it was matched at Travemünde against the similarly powered Bf 109 prototype, as well as the "also rans", the Ar 80 and Fw 159. Though Heinkel's fighter was marginally slower, it had better field performance, much better pilot view (especially on the ground), a wide-track landing gear and considerably better manoeuvrability. Many, especially Heinkel, were amazed when the Messerschmitt design was chosen for the Luftwaffe,

Below: Six of the 30 Heinkel He 112B-0 fighters which were supplied to augment the fighter strength of the Luftwaffe during the 1938 Munich talks. A few weeks later they were exported.

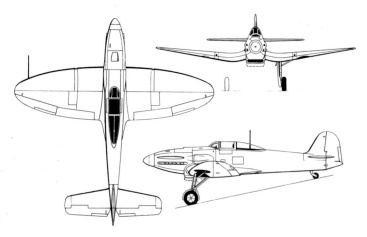

Above: Three-view of the He 112B-1 (700hp Jumo 210G).

though the He 112 was continued as an insurance. Nothing Heinkel could do with improved versions could shake the RLM's rejection, despite the delight of the RLM test pilots in flying them. Thirty He 112B-0 fighters were supplied to the Luftwaffe for evaluation, but 17 were promptly shipped to Spain (not as part of the Legion Kondor but flown by volunteer civilians). There they were judged superior to the Bf 109C, and 15 continued in Spanish service until after World War II. All but one of the other Luftwaffe machines were sold to the Japanese Navy, which disliked them intensely because of their high wing loading. Romania bought 13 B-0 and 11 B-1 fighters in 1939 and used them in the 1941 invasion of the Soviet Union.

Left: Though it was a shapely fighter, the He 112 had a shallow canopy and all-round visibility was not good. This aircraft was an He 112B-0 of III/JG 132 at Fürstenwalde in September 1938. The coolant radiator is shown fully extended (broken line in three-view).

Below: The civil-registered batch of 12 Heinkel He 112B-0 fighters lined up at Rostock-Marienehe before shipment to Japan in May 1938. The second batch was temporarily diverted to the Luftwaffe.

Heinkel He 162 Salamander

He 162A-2

Origin: Ernst Heinkel AG; first batch Vienna-Schwechat, production totally dispersed with underground assembly at Nordhausen (Mittelwerke), Bernberg (Junkers) and Rostock (Heinkel).

Type: Single-seat interceptor.

Engine: One 1,760lb (800kg) thrust BMW 003E-1 or E-2 Orkan single-shaft turbojet.

Dimensions: Span 23ft 7¾in (7·2m); length 29ft 8½in (9m); height 6ft 6½in (2–6m).

Weights: Empty 4,796lb (2180kg); loaded 5,940lb (2695kg).

Performance: Maximum speed 490mph (784km/h) at sea level, 522mph (835km/h) at 19,700ft (6000m); initial climb 4,200ft (1280m)/min; service ceiling 39,500ft (12,040m); range at full throttle 434 miles (695km) at altitude.

Armament: Early versions, two 30mm Rheinmetall MK 108 cannon with 50 rounds each; later production, two 20mm Mauser MG 151/20 with 120 rounds each.

History: First flight 6 December 1944; first delivery January 1945.

User: Germany (Luftwaffe).

Development: Popularly called "Volksjäger" (People's Fighter), this incredible aircraft left behind so many conflicting impressions it is hard to believe the whole programme was started and finished in little more than six months. To appreciate the almost impossible nature of the programme, Germany was being pounded to rubble by fleets of Allied bombers that darkened the sky, and the aircraft industry and the Luftwaffe's fuel supplies were inexorably running down. Experienced aircrew had nearly all been killed, materials were in critically short supply and time had to be measured

Below: This He 162A-2 was one of about 50 that reached Parchim by March 1945 for converting pilots of I/JG 1.

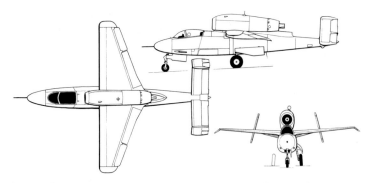

Above: Three-view of the mass-produced He 162A-2 Salamander.

not in months but in days. So on 8 September 1944 the RLM issued a specification calling for a 750km/h jet fighter to be regarded as a piece of consumer goods and to be ready by 1 January 1945. Huge numbers of workers were organised to build it even before it was designed and Hitler Youth were hastily trained in primary gliders before being strapped into the new jet. Heinkel, which had built the world's first turbojet aircraft (He 178, flown 27 August 1939) and the first jet fighter (He 280 twin-jet, flown on its jet engines 2 April 1941) won a hasty competition with a tiny wooden machine with its engine perched on top and blasting between twin fins. Drawings were ready on 30 October 1944. The prototype flew in 37 days and plans were made for production to rise rapidly to 4,000 per month. Despite extreme difficulties, 300 of various sub-types had been completed by VE-day, with 800 more on the assembly lines. I/JG1 was operational at Leck, though without fuel. Despite many bad characteristics the 162 was a fighter of a futuristic kind, created in quantity far quicker than modern aircraft are even drawn on paper.

Below: Some idea of what was accomplished in seven weeks is shown by this view of one of the many He 162A assembly shops, in this case a former salt mine at Tarthun. This remarkable fighter still looks modern today, but in fact it was much too advanced for Hitler Youth pilots.

Heinkel He 219 Uhu

He 219A-0 to A-7, B and C series

Origin: Ernst Heinkel AG.
Type: A series, two-seat night fighter.
Engines: Usually two 1,900hp Daimler-Benz DB 603G inverted-vee-12 liquid-cooled; other engines, see text.
Dimensions: (A-series) span 60ft 2in or 60ft 8in (18·5m); length (with aerials) 50ft 11¾in (15·54m); height 13ft 5½in (4·1m).
Weights: (A-7) empty 24,692lb (11,200kg); loaded 33,730lb (15,200kg).
Performance: (A-7) maximum speed 416mph (670km/h); initial climb 1,804ft (550m)/min; service ceiling 41,660ft (12,700m); range 1,243 miles (2000km).
Armament: Varied, see text.
History: First flight (219V-1) 15 November 1942; service delivery (prototypes) May 1943; (production 219A-1) November 1943.
User: Germany (Luftwaffe).

Development: Ernst Heinkel was the pioneer of gas-turbine jet aircraft, flying the He 178 on 27 August 1939 and the He 280 twin-jet fighter as a glider on 22 September 1940 and with its engines on 2 April 1941 (before the purely experimental Gloster E.28/39). But Heinkel was unable to build the extremely promising He 280 in quantity, which was fortunate for the Allies. He had no spare capacity for the He 219 either, which had excited little official interest when submitted as the P.1060 project in August 1940 as a high-speed fighter, bomber and torpedo carrier. It was only when RAF night attacks began to hurt, at the end of 1941, that he was asked to produce the 219 as a night fighter (Uhu meaning Owl). The He 219V-1, with 1,750hp DB 603AS and two MG 151/20 cannon, plus an MG 131 in the rear cockpit, was fast and extremely manoeuvrable and the test pilots at Rechlin were thrilled by it. Successive prototypes had much heavier armament and radar and 100 were ordered from five factories in Germany, Poland and Austria. The order was soon trebled and Luftwaffe enthusiasm was such that even the early prototypes were sent to Venlo, Holland, to form a special trials unit. The first six night sorties resulted in the claimed destruction of 20 RAF bombers, six of them the previously almost immune Mosquitoes! More ▶

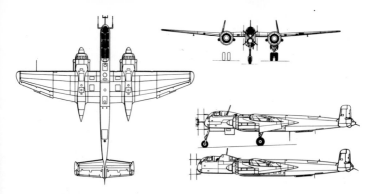

Above: Three-view of He 219A-5/R1; lower side view, the lengthened A-5/R4 with MG 131 in the rear cockpit for defence.

Above: An He 219A-5/R2 after capture of its airfield in 1945.

Below: The He 219A-7/R4 was one of the fastest and highest-flying versions, with ejection seats, but only four MG 151 forward-firing guns. Note the simplified late-war national marking.

Above: The He 219 V5 (fifth prototype) was the first to eliminate a previous unsightly step in the top of the fuselage.

than 15 different versions of the 219 then appeared, immediately proving outstandingly formidable. The A-2/R1 had 603As, two MG 151/20 in the wing roots and two or four in a belly tray and two 30mm MK 108 firing upward at 65° in a Schräge Musik (Jazz Music) installation for destroying bombers by formating below them. The A-7/R1 had MK 108s in the wing roots and two of these big guns and two MG 151/20 in the tray, plus the Schräge Musik with 100 rounds per gun (the most lethal of all). Some versions had three seats, long-span wing and DB 603L turbocharged engines, or Jumo 213s or even the 2,500hp Jumo 222 with six banks of four cylinders. The B and C families would have been enlarged multi-role versions with rear turrets. Total A-type production was only 268, the officials at one time ignoring Luftwaffe enthusiasm by ordering production to be stopped!

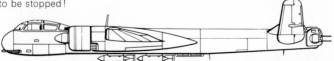

Above: The He 219C-2 Jagdbomber (fighter-bomber) would have had Jumo 222 engines and many other changes including a rear turret.

Below: This He 219A-5 appears to have a black-painted underside to its right wing; it carries both SN-2 and C-1 nose radars.

Heinkel He 280

He 280 V1 to V8

Origin: Ernst Heinkel AG.
Type: Single-seat fighter.
Engines: (Most) two 1,852lb (840kg) thrust Junkers Jumo 004A turbojets.
Dimensions: Span 39ft 4¼in (12·00m); length (most) 33ft 5½in (10·20m); height 10ft 5¾in (3·19m).
Weights: (V6) empty 7,386lb (3350kg); loaded 11,465lb (5200kg).
Performance: (V6) maximum speed 508mph (817km/h); range at height 382 miles (615km).

Development: A truly remarkable achievement, the He 280 was the world's first jet combat aircraft, the first twin-jet and the first jet to be other than a research aircraft. Yet it emerged at a time when the German leaders had a fixation on a brief Blitzkrieg victory, and showed no interest in jets or anything else that could not be used at once. The He 280 V1 was complete in September 1940 and flew as a glider on the 11th of that month behind an He 111. Fritz Schäfer then flew it on two 1,290lb (585kg) thrust HeS 8A centrifugal jets on 2 April 1941. Eventually eight of these attractive twin-finned machines were flown, but they came to nothing—despite Heinkel arranging a mock dogfight with an Fw 190 in early 1942 which the jet won easily. Intended armament was three 20mm MG 151; the proposed He 280B would have had six, plus 1,102lb (500kg) bomb load. Trials completed included twin Argus 014 duct propulsion, glider tests with no engine nacelles, and V-type butterfly tails.

Right: The first takeoff under power, on 2 April 1941. Prior to this date the only jet aircraft to have flown was the He 178.

Below: The first landing; the engine cowlings were left off to avoid build-up of dripping fuel, with consequent fire hazard.

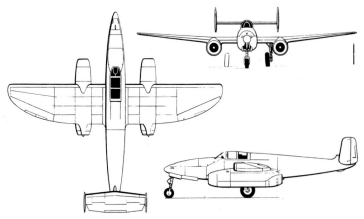

Above: Three-view of the He 280 V2, with Jumo 004 engines.

Henschel Hs 123

Hs 123A-1

Origin: Henschel Flugzeugwerke AG.
Type: Single-seat dive bomber and close-support.
Engine: One 880hp BMW 132 Dc nine-cylinder radial.
Dimensions: Span 34ft 5½in (10·5m); length 27ft 4in (8·3m) height 10ft 6½in (3·2m).
Weights: Empty 3,316lb (1504kg); loaded 4,888lb (2217kg).
Performance: Maximum speed 214mph (345km/h); initial climb 2,950ft (900m)/min; service ceiling 29,530 ft (9000m); range 530 miles (850km).
Armament: Two 7·92mm Rheinmetall MG 17 machine guns ahead of pilot; underwing racks for four 110lb (50kg) bombs, or clusters of anti-personnel bombs or two 20mm MG FF cannon.
History: First flight, spring 1935 (public display given 8 May); first delivery (Spain) December 1936; final delivery, October 1938.
User: Germany (Luftwaffe).

Development: Though representing a class of aircraft generally considered obsolete by the start of World War II, this trim little biplane was kept hard at work until 1942, achieving results which in retrospect seem almost unbelievable. The prototype needed extensive modification to produce the A-1 production version, which was tested in the Spanish Civil War. Contrary to the staff-college theories then adhered to by the newly formed Luftwaffe, the Henschels were able to give close support to ground troops of a most real and immediate kind, strafing and bombing with great accuracy despite the lack of any radio link or even an established system of operation. Eventually the Luftwaffe realised that the concept of a close-support aircraft was valid. and a few Henschels were allowed to operate in this role, but all the effort and money was put into the Ju 87, and the Hs 123 was phased out of production before World War II. Yet in the Polish campaign these aircraft proved unbelievably useful, having the ability to make pinpoint attacks with guns and bombs and, by virtue of careful setting of the propeller speed, to make a demoralising noise. Moreover, it established an extraordinary reputation for returning to base even after direct hits by AA shells. As a result, though the whole force was incessantly threatened with disbandment

Above right: An Hs 123A-1 pictured (possibly with Schlacht/LG 2) during the Blitzkrieg through the Low Countries in May 1940.

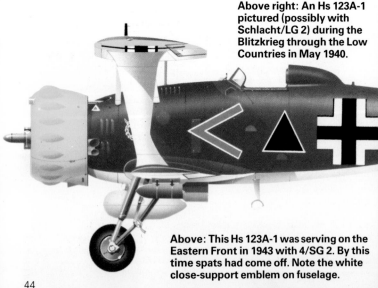

Above: This Hs 123A-1 was serving on the Eastern Front in 1943 with 4/SG 2. By this time spats had come off. Note the white close-support emblem on fuselage.

44

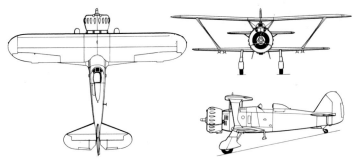

Above: Three-view of the Hs 123A-1.

or replacement by later types, the Hs 123 close-support unit II (Schlacht)/ LG2 was sent intact to the Balkans in April 1941 and thence to the USSR. Here the old biplanes fought around the clock, proving far better adapted to the conditions than more modern types and continuing in front-line operations until, by the end of 1944, there were no more left.

Right: A front-line photo taken deep in the USSR in 1942. The Polish campaign taught the Luftwaffe that close-support aircraft had to be clearly marked with large national insignia.

Henschel Hs 129

Hs 129A and B series

Origin: Henschel Flugzeugwerke AG.
Type: Single-seat close support and ground attack.
Engines: (B-series) two 690hp Gnome-Rhône 14M 04/05 14-cylinder two-row radials.
Dimensions: Span 46ft 7in (14·2m); length 31ft 11¾in (9·75m); height 10ft 8in (3·25m).
Weights: (Typical B-1) empty 8,940lb (4060kg); loaded 11,265lb (5110kg).
Performance: (Typical B-1) maximum speed 253mph (408km/h); initial climb 1,390ft (425m)/min; service ceiling 29,530ft (9000m); range 547 miles (880km).
Armament: See text.
History: First flight (Hs 129V-1) early 1939; service delivery (129A-0) early 1941; first flight (129B) October 1941; service delivery (129B) late 1942.
Users: Germany (Luftwaffe), Hungary, Romania.

Development: Though there were numerous types of specialised close support and ground attack aircraft in World War I, this category was virtually ignored until the Spanish Civil War showed, again, that it is one of the most important of all. In 1938 the RLM issued a specification for such an aircraft – the whole purpose of the Luftwaffe being to support the Wehrmacht in Blitzkrieg-type battles – to back up the purpose-designed Ju 87 dive bomber. Henschel's Dipl-Ing F. Nicholaus designed a trim machine somewhat resembling the twin-engined fighters of the period but with more armour and less-powerful engines (two 495hp Argus As 410A-1 air-cooled inverted-vee-12s). The solo pilot sat in the extreme nose behind a windscreen 3in thick, with armour surrounding the cockpit. The triangular-section fuselage housed self-sealing tanks, guns in the sloping sides and a hardpoint for a bomb underneath. Test pilots at Rechlin damned the A-0 pre-production batch as grossly underpowered, but these aircraft were used on the Eastern Front by the Romanian Air Force. The redesigned B-series used the vast

Below: This Hs 129B-2 was operating on the Russian Front with 4(Pz)/SchG 1 in 1942.

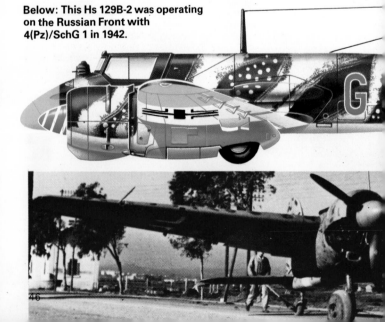

46

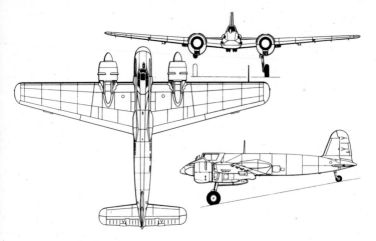

Above: Three-view of Hs 129B-1/R4 with bomb kit.

numbers of French 14M engines that were available and in production by the Vichy government for the Me 323. Altogether 841 B-series were built, and used with considerable effect on the Eastern Front but with less success in North Africa. The B-1/R1 had two 7·92mm MG 17 and two 20mm MG 151/20, plus two 110lb or 48 fragmentation bombs. The R2 had a 30mm MK 101 clipped underneath and was the first aircraft ever to use a 30mm gun in action. The R3 had a ventral box of four MG 17. The R4 carried up to 551lb of bombs. The R5 had a camera for vertical photography. The B-2 series changed the inbuilt MG 17s for MG 131s and other subtypes had many kinds of armament including the 37mm BK 3·7 and 75mm BK 7·5 with muzzle about eight feet ahead of the nose. The most novel armament, used against Russian armour with results that were often devastating, was a battery of six smooth-bore 75mm tubes firing recoilless shells down and to the rear with automatic triggering as the aircraft flew over metal objects.

Below: This Hs 129B-1 was one of the first of this type to reach the front line. Assigned to 8/Schlacht-geschwader 2 it was photographed near Tripoli in late 1942. It is being towed from each landing gear by a vehicle out of the picture, with a man steering the tailwheel. The lower half of each cowling is missing, no ventral gun is fitted and the ladder is out.

Henschel Hs 132

Hs 132 V1, V2 and A, B and C

Origin: Henschel Flugzeugwerke AG.
Type: Dive bomber.
Engine: 1,760lb (800kg) thrust BMW 003A-1 turbojet.
Dimensions: Span 23ft 7½in (7·20m); length 29ft 2½in (8·90m); height 9ft 10in (3·00m).
Weights: Empty, not known; loaded 7,496lb (3400kg).
Performance: Maximum speed (with bomb) 435mph (700km/h), (clean) 485mph (780km/h); range (with bomb, at 32,800ft, 10,000m) 696 miles (1120km).
Development: In 1937 the DVL research into dive bombing led to the Berlin-Charlottenberg B9 being built to study the advantages of the pilot lying prone, to better resist g forces. Extensive B9 testing throughout World War II showed how great the advantages were, and it was also clear that frontal area could be reduced. This led to the Henschel Hs 132 prone-pilot dive bomber, begun in early 1944. The 132A-series were to be dive bombers

Junkers Ju 87

Ju 87A, B and D series

Origin: Junkers Flugzeug und Motorenwerke AG; also built by Weser Flugzeugbau and components from SNCASO, France.
Type: Two-seat dive bomber and ground attack.
Engine: (Ju 87B-1) one 1,100hp Junkers Jumo 211Da 12-cylinder inverted-vee liquid-cooled; (Ju 87D-1, D-5) 1,300hp Jumo 211J.
Dimensions: Span (Ju 87B-1, D-1) 45ft 3¼in (13·8m); (D-5) 50ft 0½in (15·25m); length 36ft 5in (11·1m); height 12ft 9in (3·9m).
Weights: Empty (B-1, D-1) about 6,080lb (2750kg); loaded (B-1) 9,371lb (4250kg); (D-1) 12,600lb (5720kg); (D-5) 14,500lb (6585kg).
Performance: Maximum speed (B-1) 242mph (390km/h); (D-1) 255mph (408km/h); (D-5) 250mph (402km/h); service ceiling (B-1) 26,250ft (8000m); (D-1, D-5) 24,000ft (7320m); range with maximum bomb load (B-1) 373 miles (600km); (D-1, D-5) 620 miles (1000km). ***continued ▶***

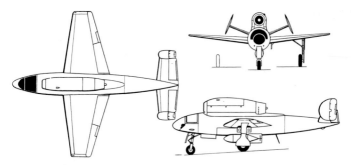

Above: Three-view of Hs 132A with 500kg bomb.

with 1,102lb (500kg) bomb but no guns. The 132B, with Jumo 004 engine, was to carry a similar bomb as well as two 20mm MG 151 cannon. It was believed Allied AA gunners would be unable to hit so small an aircraft diving at over 500mph. There were other projected versions, but the Soviet army occupied the factory just as the V1 was about to begin flight testing.

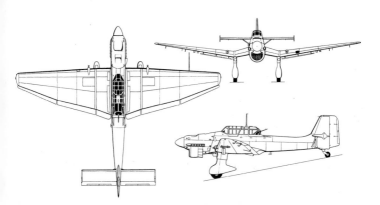

Above: Three-view of Ju 87B-2, without bombs.

Left: This Ju 87D-1/Trop was the aircraft of Oberstleutnant Walter Sigel, Geschwaderkommodore (wing commander) of Stukageschwader 3, at Derna, Libya, in June 1942. The much better shape of this later version can be seen by comparison with the three-view above. The aircraft is shown with a 500kg (1,102lb) bomb on the main crutch and twin MG 81 at the rear. The cylinder projecting horizontally ahead of the landing gear is a wind-driven siren.

Armament: (Ju 87B-1) two 7·92mm Rheinmetall MG 17 machine guns in wings, one 7·92mm MG 15 manually aimed in rear cockpit, one 1,102lb (500kg) bomb on centreline and four 110lb (50kg) on wing racks; (D-1, D-5) two MG 17 in wings, twin 7·92mm MG 81 machine guns manually aimed in rear cockpit, one bomb of 3,968lb (1800kg) on centreline; (D-7) two 20mm MG 151/20 cannon in wings; (Ju 87G-1) two 37mm BK (Flak 18, or Flak 36) cannon in underwing pods; (D-4) two underwing WB81 weapon containers each housing six MG 81 guns.

History: First flight (Ju 87V1) late 1935; (pre-production Ju 87A-0) November 1936; (Ju 87B-1) August 1938; (Ju 87D-1) 1940; termination of production 1944.

Users: Bulgaria, Croatia, Germany (Luftwaffe), Hungary, Italy, Romania, Slovakia.

Development: Until at least 1942 the Ju 87 "Stuka" enjoyed a reputation that struck terror into those on the ground beneath it. First flown with a British R-R Kestrel engine and twin fins in 1935, it entered production in 1937 as the Ju 87A with large trousered landing gear and full equipment for dive bombing, including a heavy bomb crutch that swung the missile well clear of the fuselage before release. The spatted Ju 87B was the first aircraft in production with the Jumo 211 engine, almost twice as powerful as the Jumo 210 of the Ju 87A, and it had an automatic device (almost an auto-pilot) to ensure proper pull-out from the steep dive, as well as red lines at 60°, 75° and 80° painted on the pilot's side window. Experience in Spain had shown that pilots could black-out and lose control in the pull-out. Later a whole formation of Ju 87Bs in Spain was late pulling out over misty ground and many hit the ground. In Poland and the Low Countries the Ju 87 was terribly effective and it repeated its success in Greece, Crete and parts of the Russian front. But in the Battle of Britain its casualty rate was such that it was soon withdrawn, thereafter to attack ships and troops in areas where the Axis still enjoyed some air superiority. In 1942—45 its main work was close support on the Eastern front, attacking armour with big guns (Ju 87G-1) and even being used as a transport and glider tug. Total production, all by Junkers, is believed to have been 5,709.

Though substantial numbers were built of the Ju 87A series with Jumo 210 engine, these were replaced in front-line units in 1939 by the more powerful B-series, serving thereafter until early 1943 as dive-bomber trainers. The Ju 87B was the first production application of the Jumo 211 engine, which by mid-1938 was available in improved Jumo 211Da form

Above: Flanked by a 500kg bomb, this Ju 87B-2 served with StG 77 in the Balkans and Crete, thence moving to the USSR.

rated at 1,200hp with direct fuel injection, making the engine insensitive to accelerations and flight attitudes. By the start of World War II all nine Stukagruppen had re-equipped with the Ju 87B-1, which was developed into sub-types with better radio, armour, skis, sand filters and many other improvements. Nevertheless the basic vulnerability of the Ju 87 had by this time resulted in a planned phase-out of production by 1940. Production was tapering off as the war started, but the shattering effect of the aircraft in ▶

Below: Distinguished by its two 66 Imp gal drop tanks under the outer wings, the Ju 87R family were essentially extended-range versions of the B-2. Usually restricted to a single 500kg bomb on the centreline, the R offered approximately twice the radius of action of the B-2, entering service in early 1940.

Poland caused its run-down to be postponed. In the campaign in the West in May 1940 the Stuka did even more to blast a path for the Wehrmacht, and not even its inability to survive over England was enough to stop it coming off the production line. In the spring of 1941 the greatly improved D-series thus entered production, with more power, greatly increased bomb load, extensive armour and many other changes. But the whole programme was totally unplanned. Output was always being tapered off, only to be suddenly boosted to meet urgent demands. Better aircraft kept failing to appear, Junkers themselves failed to produce the planned Ju 187, and output kept rising and falling until it at last ended in September 1944 when more than 5,700 had been delivered. Many of the final sub-types were of the G-series with tank-busting cannon, or dual-control H-series trainers. Most of the Stukas in action on the Eastern front after late 1942 had to be restricted (if possible) to night operations with large flame-damping exhaust pipes. Only a very few, flown by crews either deeply experienced or just joined, survived to VE-day. Various models served with the Slovakian, Romanian and Hungarian air forces and with the Regia Aeronautica (giving rise to the erroneous belief by the Allies it was built in Italy as the "Breda 201"), and among many special versions or modifications were fleet carrier-based models intended for *Graf Zeppelin*, glider tugs, large belly freight pods and passenger pods fitted above the wings.

Below: At the end of the war few Stukas were left in action, one of them being this Ju 87G-1 anti-tank aircraft on the Eastern Front. Unwieldy, it was very vulnerable to fighters.

Above: After Italy's entry to the war in June 1940 more than 200 Ju 87Bs were supplied to Italy's Regia Aeronautica. Britain believed there was an Italian-built 'Breda 201' version.

Junkers Ju 88

Many versions: data for Ju 88A-4, C-6, G-7, S-1

Origin: Junkers Flugzeug und Motorenwerke AG, dispersed among 14 plants with subcontract or assembly by ATG, Opel, Volkswagen and various French groups.

Type: Military aircraft designed as dive bomber but developed for level bombing, close support, night fighting, torpedo dropping, reconnaissance and as pilotless missile. Crew: two to six.

Engines: (A-4) two 1,340hp Junkers Jumo 211J 12-cylinder inverted-vee liquid-cooled; (C-6) same as A-4; (G-7) two 1,880hp Junkers Jumo 213E 12-cylinder inverted-vee liquid-cooled; (S-1) two 1,700hp BMW 801G 18-cylinder two-row radials.

Dimensions: Span 65ft 10½in (20·13m) (early versions 59ft 10¾in); length 47ft 2¼in (14·4m); (G-7, 54ft 1½in); height 15ft 11in (4·85m); (C-6) 16ft 7½in (5m).

Weights: Empty (A-4) 17,637lb (8000kg); (C-6b) 19,090lb (8660kg); (G-7b) 20,062lb (9100kg); (S-1) 18,300lb (8300kg); maximum loaded (A-4) 30,865lb (14,000kg); (C-6b) 27,500lb (12,485kg); (G-7b) 32,350lb (14,690kg); (S-1) 23,100lb (10,490kg).

Performance: Maximum speed (A-4) 269mph (433km/h); (C-6b) 300mph (480km/h); (G-7b) (no drop tank or flame-dampers) 402mph (643km/h); (S-1) 373mph (600km/h); initial climb (A-4) 1,312ft (400m)/min; (C-6b) about 985ft (300m)/min; (G-7b) 1,640ft (500m)/min; (S-1) 1,804ft (550m)/min; service ceiling (A-4) 26,900ft (8200m); (C-6b) 32,480ft (9900m); (G-7b) 28,870ft (8800m); (S-1) 36,090ft (11,000m); range (A-4) 1,112 miles (1790km); (C-6b) 1,243 miles (2000km); (G-7b) 1,430 miles (2300km); (S-1) 1,243 miles (2000km).

Armament: (A-4) two 7.92mm MG 81 (or one MG 81 and one 13mm MG 131) firing forward, twin MG 81 or one MG 131 upper rear, one or two MG 81 at rear of ventral gondola and (later aircraft) two MG 81 at front of gondola; (C-6b) three 20mm MG FF and three MG 17 in nose and two 20mm MG 151/20 firing obliquely upward in Schräge Musik installation; (G-7b) four MG 151/20 (200 rounds each) firing forward from ventral

Below: Most Ju 88 night fighters had BMW 801 radial engines, but the G-7a of late 1944 had Jumo 213 engines. Note SN-2 nose radar.

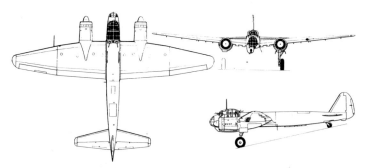

Above: Three-view of the first long-span version, the A-4.

fairing, two MG 151/20 in Schräge Musik installation (200 rounds each) and defensive MG 131 (500 rounds) swivelling in rear roof; (S-1) one MG 131 (500 rounds) swivelling in rear roof; bomb loads (A-4) 1,100lb (500kg) internal and four external racks rated at 2,200lb (1000kg) (inners) and 1,100lb (500kg) (outers) to maximum total bomb load of 6,614lb (3000kg); (C-6b and G-7b, nil); (S-1) up to 4,410lb (2000kg) on external racks.

History: First flight (Ju 88V1) 21 December 1936; (first Ju 88A-1) 7 September 1939; (first fighter, Ju 88C-0) July 1939; (Ju 88C-6) mid-1942; (first G-series) early 1944; (S series) late 1943; final deliveries, only as factories were overrun by Allies.

Users: Bulgaria (briefly), Finland, Germany (Luftwaffe), Hungary, Italy, Romania.

Development: Probably no other aircraft in history has been developed in so many quite different forms for so many purposes — except, perhaps, for the Mosquito. Flown long before World War II as a civil prototype, after a rapid design process led by two temporarily hired Americans well-versed in modern stressed-skin construction, the first 88s were transformed into the heavier, slower and more capacious A-1 bombers which were just entering service as World War II began. The formidable bomb load and generally good performance were offset by inadequate defensive armament, and in the A-4 the span was increased, the bomb load and gun power substantially augmented and a basis laid for diverse further development. Though it would be fair to describe practically all the subsequent versions as a hodge-podge of ▶

Above: Side views of the Ju 88G-7a night fighter (left) and Ju 88P-1 anti-tank aircraft with jettisonable 75mm gun (right).

lash-ups, the Ju 88 was structurally excellent, combined large internal fuel capacity with great load-carrying capability, and yet was never so degraded in performance as to become seriously vulnerable as were the Dornier and Heinkel bombers. Indeed, with the BMW radial and the Jumo 213 engines the later versions were almost as fast as the best contemporary fighters at all altitudes and could be aerobatted violently into the bargain. A basic design feature was that all the crew were huddled together, to improve combat morale; but in the Battle of Britain it was found this merely made it difficult to add proper defensive armament and in the later Ju 188 a much larger crew compartment was provided. Another distinctive feature was the large single struts of the main landing gear, sprung with stacks of chamfered rings of springy steel, and arranged to turn the big, soft-field wheels through 90° to lie flat in the rear of the nacelles. In 1940 to 1943 about 2,000 Ju 88 bombers were built each year, nearly all A-5 or A-4 versions. After splitting off completely new branches which led to the Ju 188 and 388, bomber development was directed to the streamlined S series of much higher performance, it having become accepted that the traditional Luftwaffe species of bomber was doomed if intercepted, no matter how many extra guns and crew it might carry. Indeed even the bomb and fuel loads were cut in most S sub-types, though the S-2 had fuel in the original bomb bay and

Junkers Ju 388J

Ju 388L-series, J-series and K-series

Origin: Junkers Flugzeug und Motorenwerke AG.
Type: (L) Recce, (J) night fighter, (K) bomber.
Engines: (Most) two 1,890hp BMW 801TJ 18-cyl two-row radials, (some) two 1,750hp Junkers Jumo 213E inverted-vee-12 liquid-cooled.
Dimensions: Span 72ft 2in (22·00m); length (L-1) 49ft 10½in (15·20m), (J-1) 53ft 5½in (16·29m) (58ft 1in with tail-warning radar); height 14ft 3in (4·35m).
Weights: Empty (L-1) 22,810lb (10,345kg), (J-1) 22,928lb (10,400kg); loaded (L-1, J-1) 32,350lb (14,675kg).
Performance: Maximum speed at altitude (L-1) 407mph (655km/h), (J-1) 362mph (582km/h); service ceiling (typical) 44,000ft (13,500m); range (L-1, internal fuel only) 1,838 miles (2950km).

Development: Originally the Ju 188S and T, these extremely important combat aircraft began as the Hubertus project in September 1943. The only type to reach the Luftwaffe in quantity was the L-1, built by ATG at Merseburg and Weser at Bremen. This was a pressurized three-seater, and like other versions had extremely highly rated turbocharged engines giving almost full power at around 35,000ft. None of the numerous K-series got into service, but the J-1 was so good a night and all-weather fighter it continued after the cancellation of all except "emergency fighter" programmes in July 1944. Most J-series did not have the twin-MG 131 tail barbette, but typical armament included two 30mm and two MG 151 firing ahead and two MG 151 in a Schräge Musik oblique installation in the rear fuselage. Nose radar included the FuG 218 Neptun with Morgenstern (Morning Star) aerial array mostly enclosed in a plywood nosecone.

Above: One of the first of nearly 15,000 Ju 88s was this long-span A-5 of 1939, seen with two external SC250 (551lb) bombs.

large bulged bomb stowage (which defeated the objective of reducing drag). Final bomber versions included the P series of big-gun anti-armour and close-support machines, the Nbwe with flame-throwers and recoilless rocket projectors, and a large family of Mistel composite-aircraft combinations, in which the Ju 88 lower portion was a pilotless missile steered by the fighter originally mounted on top. Altogether bomber, reconnaissance and related 88s totalled 10,774, while frantic construction of night fighter versions in 1944–45 brought the total to at least 14,980. The Ju 88 night fighters (especially the properly designed G-series) were extremely formidable, bristling with radar and weapons and being responsible for destroying more Allied night bombers than all other fighters combined.

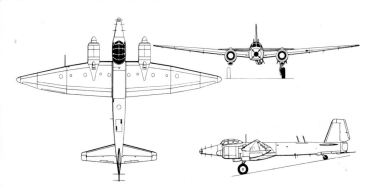

Above: Three-view of Ju 388J-1 with Neptun radar and oblique guns.

Below: The Ju 388 V2, prototype of the 388J Störtebeker (a legendary German pirate) night-fighter with SN-2 radar.

Messerschmitt Bf 109

Bf 109B, C, D, E, F, G, H and K series, S-99 and 199, Ha-1109 and -1112

Origin: Bayerische Flugzeugwerke, later (1938) renamed Messerschmitt AG; very widely subcontracted throughout German-controlled territory and built under licence by Dornier-Werke, Switzerland, and Hispano-Aviación, Spain (post-war, Avia, Czechoslovakia).

Type: Single-seat fighter (many, fighter bomber).

Engine: (B, C) one 635hp Junkers Jumo 210D inverted-vee-12 liquid-cooled; (D) 1,000hp Daimler-Benz DB 600Aa, same layout; (E) 1,100hp DB 601A, 1,200hp DB 601N or 1,300hp DB 601E; (F) DB 601E; (G) 1,475hp DB 605A-1, or other sub-type up to DB 605D rated 1,800hp with MW50 boost; (H-1) DB 601E; (K) usually 1,550hp DB 605ASCM/DCM rated 2,000hp with MW50 boost; (S-199) 1,350hp Jumo 211F; (HA-1109) 1,300hp Hispano-Suiza 12Z-89 upright vee-12 or (M1L) 1,400hp R-R Merlin 500-45.

Dimensions: Span (A to E) 32ft 4½in (9·87m); (others) 32ft 6½in (9·92m); length (B, C) 27ft 11in; (D, E, typical) 28ft 4in (8·64m); (F) 29ft 0½in; (G) 29ft 8in (9·04m); (K) 29ft 4in; (HA-1109-M1L) 29ft 11in; height (E) 7ft 5½in (2·28m); (others) 8ft 6in (2·59m).

Weights: Empty (B-1) 3,483lb; (E) 4,189lb (1900kg) to 4,421lb; (F) around 4,330lb; (G) 5,880lb (2667kg) to 6,180lb (2800kg); (K, typical) 6,000lb; maximum loaded (B-1) 4,850lb; (E) 5,523lb (2505kg) to 5,875lb (2665kg); (F-3) 6,054lb; (G) usually 7,496lb (3400kg); (K) usually 7,439lb (3375kg).

Performance: Maximum speed (B-1) 292mph; (D) 323mph; (E) 348–354 mph (560–570km/h); (F-3) 390mph; (G) 353 to 428mph (569–690km/h), (K-4) 452mph (729km/h); initial climb (B-1) 2,200ft/min; (E) 3,100 to 3,280ft (1000m)/min; (G) 2,700 to 4,000ft/min; (K-4) 4,823ft (1470m)/min; service ceiling (B-1) 26,575ft; (E) 34,450ft (10,500m) to 36,090ft (11,000m); (F, G) around 38,000ft (11,600m); (K-4) 41,000ft (12,500m); range on internal fuel (all) 365–460 miles (typically, 700km).

Right: The very first Bf 109 production variant was the B-1 which was delivered from February 1937, long before any production Hurricane or Spitfire. This example had the cropped spinner that became standard (the B-2 switched to the VDM-Hamilton variable-pitch propeller). This aircraft served with Luftkreiskommando II at Berlin in 1938.

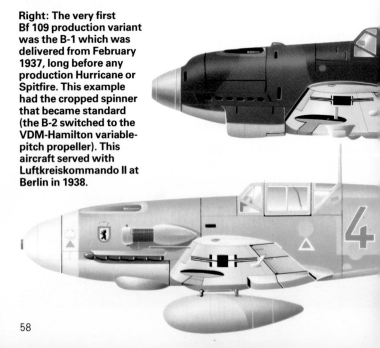

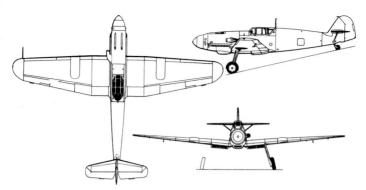

Above: Abandoned high-altitude variant, the Bf 109H of 1944.

Below: The original prototype, with British Kestrel engine.

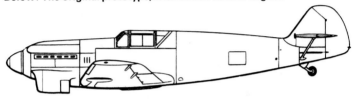

Armament: (B) three 7·92mm Rheinmetall-Borsig MG 17 machine guns above engine and firing through propeller hub; (C) four MG 17, two above engine and two in wings, with fifth through propeller hub in C-2; (early E-1) four MG 17, plus four 50kg or one 250kg (551lb) bomb; (later E-1 and most other E) two MG 17 above engine, each with 1,000 rounds (or two ▶

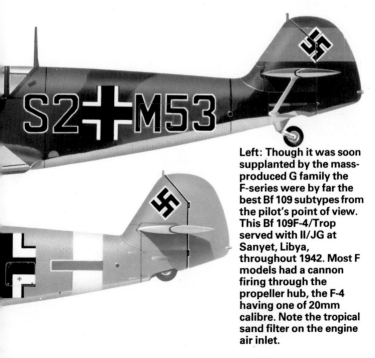

Left: Though it was soon supplanted by the mass-produced G family the F-series were by far the best Bf 109 subtypes from the pilot's point of view. This Bf 109F-4/Trop served with II/JG at Sanyet, Libya, throughout 1942. Most F models had a cannon firing through the propeller hub, the F-4 having one of 20mm calibre. Note the tropical sand filter on the engine air inlet.

Above: A frame from a propaganda film of 1941 showing two
Bf 109E-4/Trop fighters of I/JG 27 flying over Libya soon after the
formation of the Afrika Korps.

Below: One of the last of the E-series versions, this Bf 109E-7 was
photographed in 1942 flying with JG 5 on the Leningrad Front. Note the
pointed spinner and large air-inlet dust filter.

Above: These Bf 109G-6/R2 interceptors are equipped with the 210mm Wfr Gr 21 underwing mortars, firing large rockets. The weapon was a pulk-zerstörer (bomber-formation destroyer).

MG 17 with 500 rounds, plus 20mm MG FF firing through propeller hub) and two MG FF in wings, each with 60-round drum; (F-1) two MG 17 and one MG FF; (F-2) two 15mm MG 151 and one MG FF; (F-4) two MG 151, one MG FF and one 20mm MG 151 in fairing under each wing; (G-1) two MG 17 or 13mm MG 131 over engine and one MG 151; (G-6) one 30mm MK 108, two MG 131 above engine and two MG 151 under wings; (K-4) two MG 151 above engine and one MK 108 or 103; (K-6) two MG 131 above engine, one MK 103 or 108 and two MK 108 under wings; (S-199) two MG 131 above engine and two MG 151 under wings; (HA-1109 series) two wing machine guns or 20mm Hispano 404. Many German G and K carried two 210mm rocket tubes under wings or various bomb loads.

History: First flight (Bf 109 V-1) early September 1935; (production B-1) February 1937; (Bf 109E) January 1939; (Bf 109F prototype) July 1940; replacement in production by Bf 109G, May 1942.

Users: Bulgaria, Croatia, Finland, Germany (Luftwaffe), Hungary, Italy (ARSI), Japan, Jugoslavia, Romania, Slovakia, Slovak (CB Insurgent), Soviet Union (1940), Spain, Switzerland; (post-war) Czechoslovakia, Israel.

Development: During World War II the general public in the Allied nations at first regarded the Messerschmitt as an inferior weapon compared with the Spitfire and other Allied fighters. Only in the fullness of time was it possible to appreciate that the Bf 109 was one of the greatest combat aircraft in history. First flown in 1935, it was a major participant in the Spanish Civil War and a thoroughly proven combat aircraft by the time of Munich (September 1938). Early versions were the Bf 109B, C and D, all of ▶

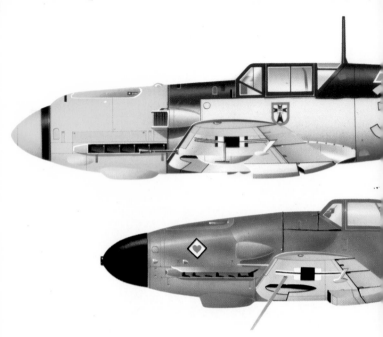

lower power than the definitive 109E. The E was in service in great quantity by the end of August 1939 when the invasion of Poland began. From then until 1941 it was by far the most important fighter in the Luftwaffe, and it was also supplied in quantity to numerous other countries (which are listed above). During the first year of World War II the "Emil", as the various E sub-types were called, made mincemeat of the many and varied types of fighter against which it was opposed, with the single exception of the Spitfire (which it greatly outnumbered). Its good points were small size, fast and cheap production, high acceleration, fast climb and dive, and good power of manoeuvre. Nearly all 109Es were also fitted with two or three 20mm cannon, with range and striking power greater than a battery of eight rifle-calibre guns. Drawbacks were the narrow landing gear, severe swing on take-off or landing, extremely poor lateral control at high speeds, and the fact that in combat the slats on the wings often opened in tight turns; while this prevented a stall, it snatched at the ailerons and threw the pilot off his aim. After 1942 the dominant version was the 109G ("Gustav") which made up over 70 per cent of the total received by the Luftwaffe. Though formidably armed and equipped, the vast swarms of "Gustavs" were nothing like such good machines as the lighter E and F, demanding constant pilot attention, constant high power settings, and having landing characteristics described as "malicious". Only a few of the extended-span high-altitude H-series were built, but from October 1944 the standard production series was the K with clear-view "Galland hood", revised wooden tail and minor structural changes. After World War II the Czech Avia firm found their Bf 109 plant intact and began building the S-99; running out of DB 605 engines they installed the slow-revving Jumo, producing the S-199 with even worse torque and swing than the German versions (pilots called it "Mezek" meaning mule), but in 1948 managed to sell some to Israel. The Spanish Hispano Aviación flew its first licence-built 1109 in March 1945 and in 1953 switched to the Merlin engine to produce the 1109-M1L Buchón (Pigeon). Several Hispano and Merlin versions were built in Spain, some being tandem-seat trainers. When the last HA-1112 flew out of Seville in late 1956 it closed out 21 years of manufacture of this classic fighter, during which total output approached 35,000.

Top of page: Not all Emils (Bf 109E-series) had a blunt spinner (with or without cannon firing through the hub); this pointed-nose E-4 served with famed I/JG 1 at De Kooy, Holland, in 1941.

Above: One of the final versions was the 1944 K-series which usually had the so-called Galland hood and a new wooden tail. This aircraft was a K-4, serving with II/JG 77 at Hopsten.

Below: This Bf 109F-4 was photographed in early 1942 whilst serving with III/JG 26 (the staffel previously commanded by Adolf Galland who until late 1941 was geschwaderkommodore of the whole JG 26 wing). The F-series kept up the pressure on the RAF's Spitfires, which were inferior in climbing and diving but in general could turn more tightly if flown with determination.

Messerschmitt Bf 110

Bf 110B series to H series
(data for Bf 110C-4/B)

Origin: Bayerische Flugzeugwerke, after 1938 Messerschmitt AG; widely dispersed manufacture.

Type: Two-seat day and night fighter (also used on occasion for ground attack and reconnaissance).

Engines: Two 1,100hp Daimler-Benz DB 601A; (later C-4s) 1,200hp DB 601N 12-cylinder inverted-vee liquid-cooled; (G, H) two 1,475hp DB 605B, same layout.

Dimensions: Span 53ft 4¾in (16·25m); length 39ft 8½in (12·1m); height 11ft 6in (3·5m).

Weights: Empty 9,920lb (4500kg); loaded 15,430lb (7000kg).

Performance: Maximum speed 349mph (562km/h) at 22,966ft (7000m); climb to 18,045ft (5500m), 8 minutes; service ceiling 32,800ft (10,000m); range 528 miles (850km) at 304mph (490km/h) at 16,400ft (5000m).

Armament: Two 20mm Oerlikon MG FF cannon and four Rheinmetall 7·92mm MG 17 machine guns fixed firing forward in nose, one 7·92mm MG 15 manually aimed machine gun in rear cockpit; C-4/B also fitted with racks under centre section for four 551lb (250kg) bombs. (G-4 night fighter) two 30mm MK 108 and two 20mm MG 151 firing forward, and two MG 151 in Schräge Musik installation firing obliquely upwards (sometimes two 7·92mm MG 81 in rear cockpit).

History: First flight (Bf 110V1 prototype) 12 May 1936; (pre-production Bf 110C-0) February 1939; operational service with Bf 110C-1, April 1939; final run-down of production (Bf 110H-2 and H-4) February 1945.

User: Germany (Luftwaffe).

Development: As in five other countries at about the same time, the Reichsluftfahrtministerium decided in 1934 to issue a requirement for a new kind of fighter having two engines and exceptional range. Called a Zerstörer ▶

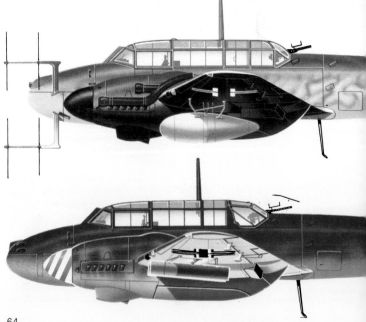

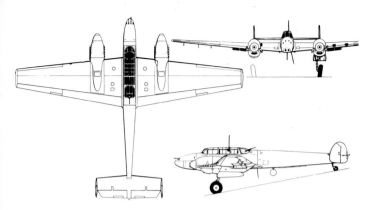

Above: Three-view of a Bf 110C-3 of early 1940.

Below: A frame from a propaganda film, this photograph shows a Bf 110D of 8/ZG 26 on escort duty from Sicily to Malta in 1942.

Left: Instead of being terminated in early 1941 production increased and by 1942 was becoming centred on night fighters. Typical of later DB 605-powered versions, this Bf 110G-4 served with 7/NJG 4 late in the war.

Left: This Bf 110G-2 served with 5/ZG 76 at Grossenhain in 1943–44. It had the larger fins, thick windscreen and other G features but was a day bomber destroyer with two Wfr Gr 21 210mm rockets under each wing.

Above: Splendid photograph of Bf 110D-1s of ZG 26 taken over the Libyan coast in 1941. The nearer aircraft wears the ZG 26 geschwader (wing) emblem and has red (8-staffel) spinners.

Below: This Bf 110C-4 of III/ZG 76 was also photographed in the Libyan desert in 1941, and has still to be painted in Sand Yellow (like the aircraft above) with white theatre band. *continued* ▶

(destroyer), it was to be as capable as small single-seaters of fighting other aircraft, possibly making up in firepower for any lack in manoeuvrability. Its dominant quality was to be range, to escort bombers on raids penetrating deep into enemy heartlands. Powered by two of the new DB 600 engines, the prototype reached 316mph, considered an excellent speed, but it was heavy on the controls and unimpressive in power of manoeuvre. Too late to be tested in the Spanish Civil War, the production Bf 110B-1, which was the first to carry the two cannon, was itself supplanted by the C-series with the later DB 601 engine with direct fuel injection and greater power at all heights. By the start of World War II the Luftwaffe had 195 Bf 110C fighters, and in the Polish campaign these were impressive, operating mainly in the close-support role but demolishing any aerial opposition they encountered. It was the same story in the Blitzkrieg war through the Low Countries and France, when 350 of the big twins were used. Only when faced with RAF Fighter Command in the Battle of Britain did the Bf 110 suddenly prove a disaster. It was simply no match for the Spitfire or even the Hurricane, and soon the Bf 109 was having to escort the escort fighters! But production of DB 605-powered versions, packed with radar and night-fighting equipment, was actually trebled in 1943 and sustained in 1944, these G and H models playing a major part in the night battles over the Reich in 1943–45.

Above: A rare photograph of the very first production version, the Bf 110A-01, at Augsburg-Haunstetten in August 1937. Powered by 680hp Jumo 210Da engines, it was slow and unimpressive.

Below: Carrying out an Rb 50/30 reconnaissance camera to a Bf 110C-5 in the Western (Libyan) desert. The 'cannon ports' are painted on.

Messerschmitt Me 210 and 410 Hornisse

Me 210A, B and C series, Me 410A and B series

Origin: Messerschmitt AG.
Type: Two-seat tactical aircraft for fighter, attack and reconnaissance duties with specialised variants.
Engines: (Me 210, usual for production versions) two 1,395hp Daimler-Benz DB 601F inverted-vee-12 liquid-cooled; (Me 410A series, usual for production versions) two 1,750hp DB 603A of same layout; (Me 410B series) two 1,900hp DB 603G.
Dimensions: Span (210) 53ft 7$\frac{1}{4}$in, later 53ft 7$\frac{3}{4}$in (16·4m); (410) 53ft 7$\frac{3}{4}$in; length (without 50mm gun, radar or other long fitment) (210) 40ft 3in (12·22m); (410) 40ft 10in or 40ft 11$\frac{1}{2}$in (12·45m); height (both) 14ft 0$\frac{1}{2}$in (4·3m).
Weights: Empty (210A) about 12,000lb (5440kg); (410A-1) 13,560lb (6150kg); maximum loaded (210A-1) 17,857lb (8100kg); (410A-1) 23,483lb (10,650kg).
Performance: Maximum speed (both, clean) 385mph (620km/h); initial climb (both) 2,133ft (650m)/min; service ceiling (210A-1) 22,967ft (7000m); (410A-1) 32,800ft (10,000m); range with full bomb load (210A-1) 1,491 miles (2400km); (410A-1) 1,447 miles (2330km).
Armament: Varied, but basic aircraft invariably defended by two remotely-controlled powered barbettes on sides of fuselage each housing one 13mm MG 131 and, if bomber version, provided with internal weapon bay housing two 1,102lb (500kg) bombs; external racks on nearly all (210 and 410) for two 1,102lb stores (exceptionally, two 2,204lb). Normal fixed forward-firing armament of two 20mm MG 151/20 and two 7·92mm MG 17. Me 410 versions had many kinds of bomber-destroyer armament, as described in the text.
History: First flight (Me 210V-1) 2 September 1939; (pre-production 210A-0) April 1941; final delivery (210) April 1942; first flight (310) 11 September 1943; (410V-1) probably December 1942.
User: Germany (Luftwaffe).

Development: Planned in 1937 as a valuable and more versatile successor to the Bf 110 twin-engined escort fighter, the Me 210 was little more than a flop and made hardly any contribution to the German war effort. After

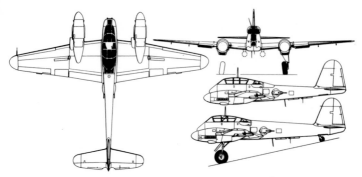

Above: Three-view of Me 210A-2 (upper side view, A-0).

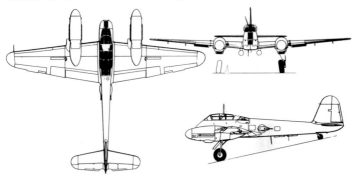

Above: Three-view of Me 410A-1 Hornisse.

severe flight instability and landing-gear problems some progress was made in 1941 towards producing an acceptable machine which could be put into production against the order for 1,000 placed "off the drawing board" in June 1939. Accidents were nevertheless frequent and manufacture was terminated at the 352nd aircraft. This major blow to the Luftwaffe and the company, which was reflected in an official demand for Willi Messerschmitt's resignation from the board, was partly salvaged by a further redesign and change to the DB 603 engine. The Me 310 was a high-

Below: This Me 410A-3 was captured by the RAF at Trapani (Sicily) in 1943; a deep-belly recon aircraft, it had served with 2(F)/122.

Top: Another Me 410A-3 of 2(F)/122 knocked out by the RAF in 1943, this one was shot down by fighters during the 8th Army's crossing of the Sangro river in Italy. **Above:** This view shows the deep fuselage of the Me 410A-3 reconnaissance version, which allowed for a proper camera installation in contrast to lash-ups used previously.

Right: Two of the last Me 210A-1s completed prior to cancellation in April 1942. Features included modified slotted wings, new rear fuselage and parallel-bar airbrakes.

altitude fighter-bomber with 58ft 9in wing and pressure cabin, but this was abandoned in favour of a less radical change designated 410. As with the 210, the reconnaissance 410s usually had cameras in the bomb bay and no MG 17s, while some attack or destroyer versions had four forward-firing MG 151 cannon, or two MG 151 and a 50mm BK 5 gun with 21 rounds. The Me 410A-2/U-2 was an important night fighter with SN-2 Lichtenstein radar and two MG 151 and two 30mm MK 108. Many of the 1,121 Me 410s carried Rüstsatz external packs housing two more MG 151, MK 108 or MK 103, and occasionally experienced pilots fitted as many as eight MG 151 all firing ahead. The 210mm rocket tube was a common fitment by 1944, some aircraft having a rotating pack of six tubes in the bomb bay.

Messerschmitt Me 163 Komet

Me 163B-1

Origin: Messerschmitt AG.
Type Single-seat interceptor.
Engine: One 3,750lb (1700kg) thrust Walter HWK 509A-2 bi-propellant rocket burning concentrated hydrogen peroxide (T-stoff) and hydrazine/methanol (C-stoff).
Dimensions: Span 30ft 7in (9·3m); length 18ft 8in (5·69m); height 9ft 0in (2·74m).
Weights: Empty 4,191lb (1905kg); loaded 9,042lb (4110kg).
Performance: Maximum speed 596mph (960km/h) at 32,800ft (10,000m); initial climb 16,400ft (5000m)/min; service ceiling 54,000ft (16,500m); range depended greatly on flight profile but under 100km (62 miles); endurance $2\frac{1}{2}$min from top of climb or eight min total.
Armament: Two 30mm MK 108 cannon in wing roots, each with 60 rounds.
History: First flight (Me 163V1) spring 1941 as glider, August 1941 under power; (Me 163B) August 1943; first operational unit (I/JG400) May 1944.
User: Germany (Luftwaffe).

Development: Of all aircraft engaged in World War II the Me 163 Komet (Comet) was the most radical and, indeed, futuristic. The concept of the short-endurance local-defence interceptor powered by a rocket engine was certainly valid and might have been more of a thorn in the Allies' side than it was. Even the dramatically unconventional form of the Me 163, with no horizontal tail and an incredibly short fuselage, did not lead to great

Top: Purging the steam-generation piping of a squadron aircraft (probably with JG 400).

Above: The first powered prototype was the Me 163A V1, which was flown as a glider in spring 1941, and with its rocket in August.

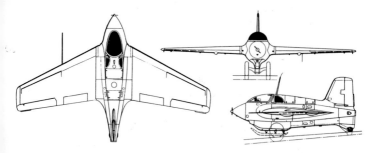

Above: Me 163B-1a showing takeoff trolley and landing skid.

difficulty; in fact, the production fighter was widely held to have the best and safest characteristics of any aircraft in the Luftwaffe. But the swift strides into uncharted technology were bold in the extreme. It was partly to save weight and drag that the tailless configuration was adopted, and partly because the moving spirit behind the project was at first Dr Alex Lippisch, who liked tailless designs. Choice of two rocket propellants that reacted violently when they came into contact solved the problem of ignition in the combustion chamber but added an extremely large element of danger. Moreover, the 163 had no landing gear, taking off from a jettisoned trolley and landing on a sprung skid, and the landing impact often sloshed residual propellants together causing a violent explosion. Many aircraft were lost this way, and the original test pilot, glider champion Heini Dittmar, was badly injured when the skid failed to extend. Nevertheless by 1944 these bat-like specks were swooping on US bomber formations with devastating effect. Numerous improved versions were flying at VE day, but only 370 Komets had seen service and these had suffered high attrition through accidents.

The roots of the project went back to the 1920s, with both Lippisch aero-dynamics and the various rocket research projects that led to the Hellmuth Walter development of engines suitable for manned aircraft from 1936. It is worth emphasizing that nothing remotely like either the airframe or the engine was attempted in Britain, nor in any other country except the Soviet Union. The early aircraft research was centred at the DFS (German sailplane research institute), where the first tailless rocket aircraft was planned as the DFS 194. In March 1938 the design was complete, but in January 1939 it was transferred to Messerschmitt. Shortly after this the Walter R I-203 rocket flew (very badly) in the He 176 research aircraft. Results with this aircraft were poor, but when a similar motor was fitted to the DFS 194 tailless aircraft ▶

Below: An Me 163B-1a Komet of II/JG 400 based at Brandis. Many were mottled grey/grey-violet/ light blue.

the speed reached 342mph (550km/h) and climb was fantastic. Swiftly sanction for a rocket fighter was gained, and gliding trials with the Me 163 V1 began in the spring of 1941. Again the tailless machine floated like a bird (the main snag being that instead of landing where the pilot wanted, it kept floating) and in July–September 1941 Dittmar pushed the speed under rocket power higher and higher, far beyond the world speed record until, on 2 October 1941, he reached about 1004km/h (623·85mph), a speed measured by theodolites on the ground. At all times the flight characteristics of all 163 versions were exemplary, but there were countless snags and

Above: One of the very first of the true production Komets, this Me 163B-1a was assigned to Ekdo (Erprobungskommando) 16 at Zwischenahn experimental airfield in July 1944. This unit worked out the training and operational tactics and procedures for the 163.

Left: Most of the operational Komets were painted in one of the various late-war colour schemes similar to this Me 163B01a used by JG 400 at Brandis in early 1945. The nose windmill drove the electric generator.

catastrophes due to the dangerous propellants, the failure of hydraulics, the extreme difficulty of taking off exactly into wind on the unsprung dolly, and the equally rigorous constraints upon the pilot in landing. Everything had to be exactly right, because if the aircraft yawed, swung or ran too far on to rough ground, it would turn over and the propellants explode.

The final developments were the Me 163C, with fully retractable tail-wheel, long body of improved form, increased-span centre section and new motor with a small chamber to give 660lb (300kg) for cruising flight, and the derived Me 263.

Messerschmitt Me 262

Me 262A-1a Schwalbe, Me 262A-2 Sturmvogel, Me 262B-1a

Origin: Messerschmitt AG.

Type: (A-1a) single-seat fighter, (A-2a) single-seat bomber, (262B-1a) two-seat night fighter.

Engines: Two 1,980lb (900kg) thrust Junkers Jumo 004B single-shaft axial turbojets.

Dimensions: Span 40ft 11½in (12·5m); length 34ft 9½in (10·6m), (262B-1a, excluding radar aerials) 38ft 9in (11·8m); height 12ft 7in (3·8m).

Weights: Empty (A-1a, A-2a) 8,820lb (4000kg); (B-1a) 9,700lb (4400kg); loaded (A-1a, A-2a) 15,500lb (7045kg); (B-1a) 14,110lb (6400kg).

Performance: Maximum speed (A-1a) 540mph (870km/h); (A-2a, laden) 470mph (755km/h); (B-1a) 497mph (800km/h); initial climb (all) about 3,940ft (1200m)/min; service ceiling 37,565ft (11,500m); range on internal fuel, at altitude, about 650 miles (1050km).

Armament: (A-1a) four 30mm MK 108 cannon in nose, two with 100 rounds each, two with 80; (A-1a/U1) two 30mm MK 103, two MK 108 and two 20mm MG 151/20; (A-1b) as A-1a plus 24 spin-stabilised R4/M 50mm rockets; (B-1a) as A-1a; (B-2a) as A-1a plus two inclined MK 108 behind cockpit in Schräge Musik installation; (D) SG 500 Jagdfaust with 12 rifled mortar barrels inclined in nose; (E) 50mm MK 114 gun or 48 R4/M rockets; bomb load of two 1,100lb (500kg) bombs carried by A-2a.

History: First flight (262V1 on Jumo 210 piston engine) 4 April 1941; (262V3 on two Jumo 004-0 turbojets) 18 July 1942; (Me 262A-1a) 7 June 1944; first delivery (A-0 to Rechlin) May 1944; first experimental combat unit (EK 262) 30 June 1944; first regular squadron (8/ZG26) September 1944.

User: Germany (Luftwaffe). **continued ▶**

Above: The Me 262A No 130 083 was redesignated V83 and test-flown with a 50mm BK 5 gun.

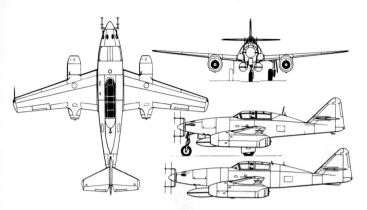

Above: Three-view of the first night-fighter version, the B-1a, rebuilt from the A-1a with SN-2 radar and a rear-seat radar operator, which was briefly operational against RAF Mosquito night intruders. Lower side view, the optimised Me 262B-2a.

Above: Starting engines of an Me 262A-1a of the Kommando Nowotny in late October 1944 (probably at Achmer).

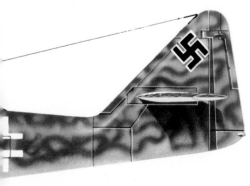

Left: One version of Me 262 to reach Luftwaffe was this Me 262A-1a/U3, an unarmed photo-reconnaissance conversion of the standard fighter which served with Einsatzkommando Braunegg in northern Italy in March 1945. Two oblique cameras (Rb 50/30s or a 20/30 and a 75/30) caused projecting bulges.

Above: This Me 262A-1a, Nr 110 025, was delivered to the first Me 262 combat unit, Kommando Nowotny, which became operational on 3 October 1944 (RAF 616 Sqn had Meteors in July).

Development: In the Me 262 the German aircraft industry created a potentially war-winning aircraft which could have restored to the Luftwaffe command of the skies over Germany. Compared with Allied fighters of its day, including the RAF Meteor I, which entered service a little earlier, it was much faster and packed a much heavier punch. Radar-equipped night fighter versions and sub-types designed to stand off from large bomber formations and blast them out of the sky were also developments against which the Allies had no answer. Yet for years the programme was held back by official disinterest, and by the personal insistence of Hitler that the world-beating jet should be used only as a bomber! It was in the autumn of 1938 that Messerschmitt was asked to study the design of a jet fighter, and the resulting Me 262 was remarkably unerring. First flown on a piston engine in the nose, it then flew on its twin turbojets and finally, in July 1943, the fifth development aircraft flew with a nosewheel. Despite numerous snags, production aircraft were being delivered in July 1944 and the rate of production was many times that of the British Meteor. On the other hand the German axial engines were unreliable and casualties due to engine failure, fires or break-up were heavy. The MK 108 gun was also prone to jam, and the landing gear to collapse. Yet the 262 was a beautiful machine to handle and, while Allied jets either never reached squadrons or never engaged enemy aircraft, the 100 or so Me 262s that flew on operations and had fuel available destroyed far more than 100 Allied bombers and fighters. Even more remarkable, by VE-day total deliveries of this formidable aircraft reached 1,433.

Below: An Me 262A-2a Sturmvogel bomber, with its two 500kg bombs in place. The first A-2a unit was III/KG 51, which became operational at Hopsten, near Rheine, on 5 October 1944.

Messerschmitt Me 263

Me 163D and 263A (Ju 248)

Origin: Messerschmitt AG; transferred to Junkers.
Type: Interceptor.
Engine: Walter HWK 109-509C-4 rocket with 3,750lb (1700kg) main chamber and 660lb (300kg) cruise chamber.
Dimensions: Span 31ft 2in (9·50m); length 25ft 10½in (7·88m); height 8ft 10¼in (2·70m).
Weights: Empty 4,640lb (2105kg); loaded 11,354lb (5150kg).
Performance: Maximum speed 620mph (1000km/h) at height; time to 49,213ft (15,000m) 3 min; max endurance, about 1hr including 15min under power.

Development: In retrospect the Me 163 need not have suffered from its most serious faults, and the 263 emerged on the Lippisch/Messerschmitt drawing boards in winter 1943–44 to rectify them. The new design had a larger and better-shaped body housing more propellants, a new engine with separate low-thrust cruise chamber for long endurance, and a proper landing gear. The 163D V1 was completed in spring 1944 but the RLM transferred the programme to Junkers to ease Messerschmitt's burdens. At Dessau Prof Hertel improved the 263A-1 into the Ju 248, with automatic slats, bubble hood and cut-down rear fuselage, larger flaps and other changes. Two 30mm

Messerschmitt Me 328

Me 328 V1, A-series and B-series

Origin: Messerschmitt AG; development and prototypes by DFS, and pre-production aircraft by Jacob Schweyer.
Type: See text.
Engines: See text.
Dimensions: Span (small) 20ft 11¾in (6·40m), (large) 27ft 10½in (8·50m); length (most) 22ft 4¾in (6·83m), (fuselage engines) 28ft 2½in (8·63m); height (on skid) (A) 6ft 10½in (2·10m), (B) 8ft 2½in (2·50m).
Weights: Empty (B-0, B-1) 3,400lb (1542kg); loaded (A-1) 4,850lb (2200kg), (A-2) 8,378lb (3800kg), (B-1) 5,953lb (2700kg), (B-2) 10,595lb (4730kg).
Performance: Maximum speed at low level (A-1) 469mph (755km/h), (A-2) 572mph (920km/h), (B-1) 423mph (680km/h), (B-2) 367mph (590km/h).

Development: This programme, extraordinary even for Nazi Germany, began in 1941 as a parasite fighter for launch from a bomber and subsequent retrieval. After widespread research and development the V1 glider began pick-a-back tests with Do 217 as carrier in autumn 1943. Powered tests began with two 660lb (300kg) thrust As 014 pulsejets on the rear fuselage, with severe problems. Then tests were made with two ducts under the wings, some being hung as far aft as possible because the intense noise damaged the wooden airframe. The A-1 fighter had two wing ducts and the A-2 four on the fuselage; respective armament was two MG 151 and two MK 103. The work then switched to assault (some expendable) with bomb loads up to 3,087lb (1400kg), the B-1 having wing engines and the B-2 bigger ducts of 880lb (400kg) each. Takeoff was by rocket trolley, cable winch and other means. Other versions were to be catapulted from U-boats.

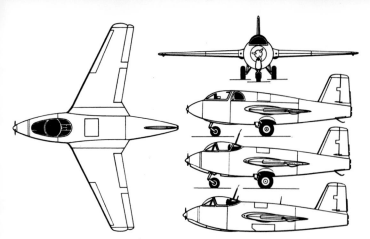

Above: Three-view of Me 263 VI (Ju 248) with upper side view as originally Me-built and lower view of proposed production 263A.

MK 108 were fitted in the wing roots. The RLM insisted on restoration of the Me 263A-1 designation, and hastened production, planning for the 5,511lb (2500kg) BMW 708 nitric-acid motor when ready, but in the chaos of late 1944 tooling was never finished, though a single Dessau-built 263A-1 flew as a glider in August 1944. It was briefly developed further by the Russians.

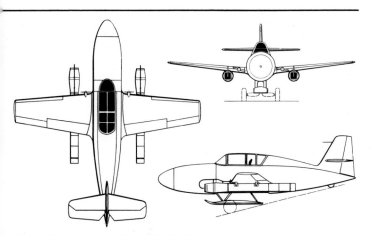

Above: Three-view of Me 328B-1 (with wing engines).
Below: One of the DFS-built towed prototypes, on skid gear.

ITALY

An observer of Italy in the 1930s would be bound to conclude that the nation was brilliant at advanced internal-combustion engines, had a flair for aircraft design and was outstanding in its aerobatic pilots. Coupled with its fascist government's top priority on military expansionism, and impressive displays of aerial power, Italy would have seemed a world leader in fighter aircraft. The exploits of the Aviazione Legionaria in the Spanish civil war reinforced this belief. Yet in World War II Italian air power, like Italian power on sea and land, was quickly regarded by Britain as a joke, a welcome light relief from the stern business of fighting Nazi Germany.

This was not due to individual lack of courage or skill on the part of Italian pilots but to many other factors of which a central one was the Italian aircraft themselves. Seeds of decline could have been discerned years earlier, in the dominant belief of the squadron pilots that manoeuvrability and pilot view mattered far more than performance or firepower, and in the abject failure of the procurement machine and industry to put sufficient effort behind the new generation of engines of much more than 1,000 horsepower. It was almost unbelievable that in June 1940, when Italy plucked up courage to join the struggle against what seemed to be enemies already defeated by Germany, virtually every one of its fighters had a Fiat A.74 engine, rated at a mere 840hp. No other major country was so crippled for lack of horsepower, and though Piaggio (for example) was flying engines of up to 1,700hp, not one got into service.

The inevitable result was a fighter force superbly equipped to

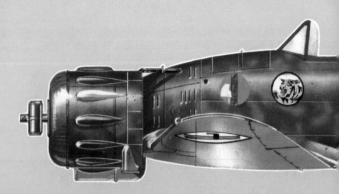

fight the battles of the pre-1937 era. The most numerous fighter was the C.R.42 biplane, a sheer delight to fly but hopelessly outclassed by Hurricanes and Spitfires. The other types available in quantity, the Fiat G.50 and Macchi C.200, were all-metal monoplanes but fitted with the same 840hp engine and same pair of 12·7mm (0·5in) machine guns. In a close dogfight fought only by ciné cameras they might have done well, but in actual warfare they were hacked out of the sky in droves.

The need for more horsepower and more firepower had been recognised well before the war, and the eventual answer was to import both from Germany. In 1939 Macchi arranged to import DB 601 engines and the first C.202 flew with such an engine in August 1940. Subsequently Fiat made the more powerful DB 605A under licence, while for firepower the extremely effective Mauser MG 151/20 cannon was adopted. The Italian industry thus had the ingredients for formidable fighters, and by all accounts the Fiat G.55, Macchi C.205 series and Reggiane Re 2005 were outstanding, with exceptional turn radius, adequate performance and considerable firepower.

In addition to these potentially staple types Italy also produced numerous other wartime fighters. Some were small and designed for economical mass production. Others were big twin-engined machines with devastating firepower, two quite dissimilar designs each having forward-firing armament of five MG 151! Another had a 1,700hp engine behind the pilot. But by 1943 Italy had lost both the capability and the will to fight, and hardly any of the good fighters were produced.

Fiat C.R.32

C.R.30, 32 and 32bis

Origin: Aeronautica d'Italia SA Fiat; built under licence by Hispano Aviaciòn, Spain.
Type: Single-seat fighter.
Engine: (C.R.30) one 600hp Fiat A.30 vee-12 water-cooled, (C.R.32) one 600hp Fiat A.30 RAbis.
Dimensions: Span (C.R. 30) 34ft 5½in (10·45m); (C.R.32) 31ft 2in (9·5m); length (30) 25ft 8¼in (7·83m); (32) 24ft 5½in (7·45m); height (30) 8ft 7½in (2·62m); (32) 7ft 9in (2·4m).
Weights: Empty (both) about 3,100lb (1400kg); loaded (both) about 4,150lb (1900kg).
Performance: Maximum speed (30) 217mph (350km/h), (32) 233mph (375km/h); initial climb (both) 2,000ft (907m)/min; service ceiling (both) about 29,530ft (9000m); range (30) 528 miles (850km), (32) 466 miles (750km).
Armament: (C.R.30) two fixed Breda-SAFAT 7·7mm or 12·7mm machine guns above engine; (C.R.32) two 12·7mm; (C.R.32bis), two 12·7mm above engine and two 7·7mm above lower wings with provision for single 220lb (100kg) or two 110lb bombs.
History: First flight (C.R.30) 1932; (C.R.32) August 1933; final delivery, about October 1939.
Users: Argentina, China, Hungary, Italy (RA), Paraguay, Spain, Venezuela.

Development: In 1923 Ing Celestino Rosatelli supervised his first C.R. (Caccia Rosatelli) fighter. From it stemmed an unbroken line which reached its climax in the 1930s. The C.R.30 offered a considerable jump in performance, for it had much more power without increase in aircraft drag. The lusty Fiat vee-12 drove a metal propeller and was cooled by a prominent circular radiator in a duct in the chin position below the crankcase. The all-metal structure was notable for continuing the scheme of Warren (W-form) interplane bracing. The tail was also braced and the main gears had large wheel spats. The C.R.32 was a general refinement, built in larger numbers and forming the major part of the Regia Aeronautica fighter force in 1935–40. In August 1936 some were sent to form La Cucaracha squadron fighting for the Spanish Nationalist forces and this grew to become by far the largest of Franco's fighter units. Spain built many under licence as the Hispano HA-132-L Chirri, and more than 150 were exported by Fiat to China, Hungary and South American countries. The nimble little Fiats were compact, robust and highly manoeuvrable and gave impressive displays all over Europe in the hands of the Pattuglie Acrobatiche. Total Fiat output amounted to at least 1,212, the final 500 being mainly four-gun 32bis fighter-bombers and a few 32ter and 32quater versions with small modifications. The Regia Aeronautica did its best with the C.R. 32 until 1942, finally using it for night tactical operations in Greece, Eritrea and Libya.

Above: This C.R.32 was used by J. G. Morato, an ace of the Spanish war.

86

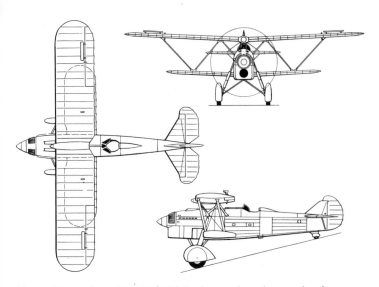

Above: Three-view of C.R.32 (32bis had guns above lower wings).

Immediately below: A C.R.32, photographed in the mid-1930s. By 1939 most had been camouflaged. Note "park bench" aileron balance visible above the upper wing.

Foot of page: The Pattuglie Acrobatiche team flew the C.R.32.

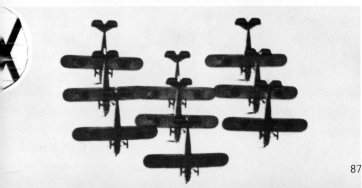

Fiat C.R.42 Falco

C.R.42, 42bis, 42ter, 42AS and 42N

Origin: Aeronautica d'Italia SA Fiat.
Type: Single-seat fighter.
Engine: One 840hp Fiat A.74 RC38 14-cylinder two-row radial.
Dimensions: Span 31ft 10in (9·7m); length 27ft 1¼in (8·25m); height 11ft 0in (3·35m).
Weights: Empty 3,790lb (1720kg); loaded 5,070lb (2300kg).
Performance: Maximum speed 267mph (430km/h); initial climb 2,400ft (732m)/min; service ceiling 34,450ft (10,500m); range 481 miles (775km).
Armament: (Early C.R.42) one 7·7mm and one 12·7mm Breda-SAFAT machine guns mounted above forward fuselage; (C.R.42bis) two 12·7mm; (C.R. 42ter) two 12·7mm and two more 12·7mm in fairings beneath lower wing; (C.R.42AS) two/four 12·7mm and underwing racks for two 220lb (100kg) bombs.
History: First flight (C.R.41) 1936; (C.R.42) January 1939; first service delivery, November 1939; termination of production, early 1942.
Users: Belgium, Finland, Hungary, Italy (RA), Sweden.

Development: In the mid-1930s the Fiat company made a firm move away from liquid-cooled vee engines and concentrated on air-cooled radials. Rosatelli prepared a fighter, the C.R.41, to take one of these, but only

Right: This C.R.42 served with the 95a Squadriglia, 18 Gruppo Caccia Terrestre, and in October 1940 was detached to Echeloo, Belgium, for missions against England. On 11 November it crossed the Suffolk coast, was intercepted and landed on the beach at Orford Ness. After testing as RAF BT 474 it was beautifully restored to its original condition at RAF St Athan and Biggin Hill.

Below: In front-line use on boggy ground many C.R.42s had their spats removed. This one in 1942 had its bomb racks loaded.

the prototype was built. Other nations were by this time (1936) giving up the open-cockpit, fabric-covered biplane in favour of the stressed-skin monoplane with retractable landing gear, but Rosatelli persisted with his C.R. family and developed the C.R.41 into the C.R.42. Though a robust, clean and very attractive design, it was really obsolete at the time of its first flight. Despite this — and perhaps confirming that Fiat knew the world market — the C.R.42 found ready acceptance. It went into large-scale production for the Regia Aeronautica and for Belgium (34, delivered January–May 1940), Hungary (at least 40, delivered December 1939–June 1940) and Sweden (72, delivered 1940–41). Total production, including the AS close support and N night fighter versions, amounted to 1,784. One group of 50 C.R.42bis provided the fighter element of the Corpo Aereo Italiano which operated from Belgium against England in October 1940–January 1941– with conspicuous lack of success. The rest persevered in the Mediterranean and North African areas, acting as both fighters and ground attack aircraft, a few being converted as dual trainers. One was built in 1940 as a twin-float seaplane and the final fling was a C.R.42B with 1,010hp DB 601A inverted-vee engine. The German power unit made it, at 323mph, the fastest biplane fighter but no production was attempted.

Below: Two C.R.42s of the 162a Squadriglia serving in North Africa. Its one asset was that it was a delight to fly.

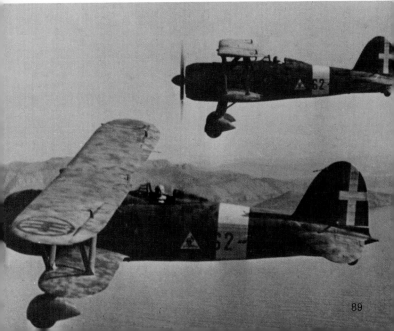

Fiat G.50 Freccia

G.50, 50bis, 50ter and 55 Centauro

Origin: Aeronautica d'Italia SA Fiat; also built by CMASA.
Type: Single-seat fighter.
Engine: (G.50, G.50bis) one 840hp Fiat A.74 RC38 14-cylinder two-row radial; (G.50ter) 1,000hp A.76 RC40S; (G.55) 1,475hp Daimler-Benz DB 605A inverted-vee-12 liquid-cooled.
Dimensions: Span, (G.50) 36ft 0in (10·97m); (G.55) 38ft 10½in (11·85m); length, (G.50) 25ft 7in (7·79m); (G.55) 30ft 9in (9.37m); height (G.50) 9ft 8in (2·9m); (G.55) 10ft 3¼in (3·15m).
Weights: Empty (G.50) 4,188lb (1900kg); (G.55) 6,393lb (2900kg); loaded (G.50) 5,966lb (2706kg); (G.55) 8,179lb (3710kg).
Performance: Maximum speed (G.50) 293mph (471km/h); (G.55) 385mph (620km/h); initial climb (G.50) 2,400ft (731m)/min; (G.55) 3,300ft (1000m)/min; service ceiling (G.50) 32,810ft (10,000m); (G.55) 42,650ft (13,000m); range (G.50) 621 miles (1000km); (G.55) 994 miles (1600km).
Armament: (G.50, G.50bis) two 12·7mm Breda-SAFAT machine guns above front fuselage; (G.55/0) as above, plus one 20mm Mauser MG 151 cannon firing through propeller hub; (G.55/I) as G.55/0 plus two 20mm MG 151 in outer wings.
History: First flight 26 February 1937; (G.50bis) September 1940; (G.55) 30 April 1942.
Users: Finland, Italy (RA, CB, ARSI), Spain.

Development: In 1935 the issue of a specification for an all-metal monoplane fighter for the Regia Aeronautica attracted at least six competing designs. Though the Macchi 200 was ultimately to become dominant, the initial winner was the Fiat G.50, the first major design by Ing Giuseppe Gabrielli (hence the designation). Its flight trials went smoothly, an order was placed in September 1937 for 45 and deliveries began early in 1938. About a dozen of the first production G.50s were sent to reinforce the Aviazione Legionaria in Spain, where their good qualities of speed and ▶

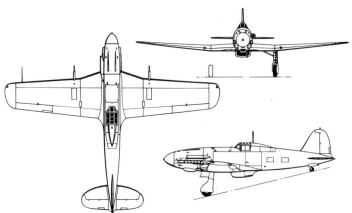

Above: Three-view of the G.55/1 with three cannon.

Below: One of the 12 G.50s from the original batch of 45 aircraft whch were sent in 1938 to the Gruppo Caccia Sperimentale in Spain. The markings are those applied in 1939, at 1° GCS based at Escalona.

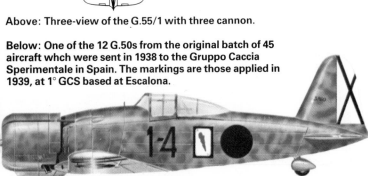

Below: M.M.5439, one of the last of the major production version, the G.50bis. This had an open-topped cockpit, broad but squat vertical tail, slotted flaps, landing gear by Magnaghi instead of Messier, and a fuel tank instead of an anti-personnel bomb bay.

Below: A swarm of Fiat G.50bis fighters serving with 51° Stormo of the Regia Aeronautica in 1941. They do not have white theatre bands and appear to be parked on a tiled apron.

Above: One of the few good photographs of a G.55, showing one of the first production machines in early 1943. It is probably fitted with a German-supplied DB 605 engine.

manoeuvrability were manifest. On the other hand pilots disliked having a sliding cockpit canopy, which was not easy to open quickly and interfered with vision, and in the next production batch of 200 an open cockpit was adopted. The poor armament was not changed, but fairings for the retracted wheels were added. Production from the CMASA plant at Marina di Pisa got under way in 1939, with deliveries replacing the C.R.32 in Regia Aeronautica fighter squadrons (not always to the pilots' delight), and a further 35 being flown to Finland in 1940 where they gave admirable service. The main production version was the G.50bis, with reprofiled fuselage giving improved pilot view, armour and self-sealing tanks. About 450 were built, mainly by CMASA. Other versions included the tandem-seat G.50B trainer, of which 139 were built; the G.50ter with more powerful engine; and prototypes of the G.50bis-A, with four 12·7mm guns and racks for two bombs, and of the DB 601A-powered G.50V.

By the time Italy entered the war in June 1940 it was obvious that the G.50 was becoming outclassed. Lack of engines of sufficient power was a major problem, but Fiat managed to obtain a Daimler-Benz DB 605A-1 from Germany and around this designed a splendid fighter with all-metal stressed-skin structure. The wing was especially efficient, and had left and right sections, each with two spars, joined on the centreline. The fuselage was well streamlined, and an enclosed cockpit was adopted without question. The prototype, called G.55 Centauro, was a vast improvement over various earlier Fiat fighters and projects using the DB 601 engine, and it flew on 30 April 1942. By January 1943 the production G.55/0 was on the line at Turin, and the 53° Stormo were delighted when they began to receive the new fighter in August 1943. Production was slow, because the Fiat RA.1050 RC58 Tifone (locally-built DB 605) was only trickling off the line, and only 105 were completed when the war ended.

Macchi M.C. 200 Saetta

M.C.200 (Serie I-XXI) and M.C.201

Origin: Aeronautica Macchi.
Type: Single-seat day fighter.
Engine: One 870hp Fiat A74RC38 14-cylinder two-row radial.
Dimensions: Span 34ft 8½in (10·58m); length 26ft 10½in (8·2m); height 11ft 6in (3·38m).
Weights: (Typical) empty 4,188lb (1900kg); (prototype) 3,902lb; (final production Serie XXI) 4,451lb; loaded 5,182lb (2350kg); (prototype) 4,850lb; (Serie XXI) 5,598lb.
Performance: Maximum speed 312mph (501km/h); initial climb 3,215ft (980m)/min; service ceiling 29,200ft (8900m); range 354 miles (570km).
Armament: Two 12·7mm Breda-SAFAT machine guns firing above engine cowling; later-Serie aircraft also had two 7·7mm in wings; M.C.200 C.B. (caccia bombardiere) had underwing racks for two bombs of up to 352lb (160kg) each, or two 33gal drop tanks.
History: First flight 24 December 1937; service delivery October 1939; final delivery, about December 1944.
User: Italy.

Development: Mario Castoldi's design team at Aeronautica Macchi, at Varese in the north Italian lakeland, was the source of the best fighters used by the Regia Aeronautica in World War II. Castoldi's staff had earlier gained great experience with high-speed aircraft with their record-breaking Schneider seaplanes, but their first monoplane fighter, the C.200, bore little evidence of this. Though a reasonably attractive stressed-skin monoplane, it had an engine of low power and the performance was correspondingly modest. Moreover it never had anything that other countries would have regarded as proper armament, though the pilot did have the advantage of cockpit indicators showing the number of rounds of ammunition unfired.

Below: M.C.200 Saettas of the initial series, with fully enclosed cockpit, based near the maker's factory at Varese in 1940.

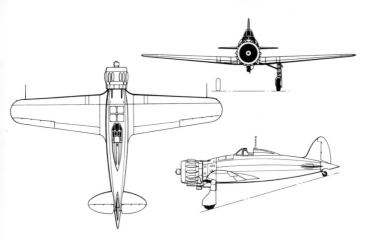

Above: Three-view of Macchi C.200 (late production serie).

Italian fighter pilots were by nature conservative; their protests caused the main production aircraft to have an open cockpit and fixed tailwheel, unlike the first batches, and combat equipment was simple in the extreme. Yet in combat with the lumbering Hurricane it proved effective, with outstanding dogfight performance and no vices. From late 1940 until Italy's surrender in September 1943 the C.200 saw more combat than any other Italian type, both around North Africa and Sicily and on the Eastern Front with the Corpo di Spedizone Italiano which claimed 88 Russian aircraft for the loss of 15 Saettas. The name Saetta, meaning lightning, refers to the lightning-bolts held by Jupiter, and is sometimes rendered as Arrow or Thunderbolt. ▶

Left: A Macchi C.200 (or M.C.200 for Mario Castoldi) of a late series in which the original sliding canopy had been replaced by a hinged hood open at the top. This one served the 90° Squadriglia, 10° Gruppo, 4° Stormo, based in Sicily in 1941. Its pilots had at first disliked the Macchi monoplanes which were instead (in 1939) first issued to the Ima Stormo.

Below: A late-series Saetta serving with the Regia Aeronautica in Italy in 1942, with (in the background) an IMAM Meridionali R.O.37 multi-role biplane, one of the most numerous types used by the Regia Aeronautica on every front during World War II.

Below: M.C.200 Saettas built by Macchi, SAI and Breda differed in many small respects, and most of the final batches had no cockpit canopy at all. There were many forms of carb-air inlet and oil cooler.

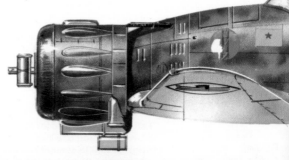

Below: This Saetta of the 373rd Squadriglia had the most common type of cockpit canopy with hinged side panels and open at the top.

Below: Takeoff by a pair of late 1943 Saettas with wings
similar to the M.C.202 with two wing machine guns.

Macchi C.202 and 205

C.202 Folgore (Lightning), C.205V Veltro (Greyhound) and C.205N Orione (Orion)

Origin: Aeronautica Macchi; production also by SAI Ambrosini and Breda.
Type: Single-seat fighter (some, fighter bomber).
Engine: (202) 1,175hp Alfa Romeo RA1000 RC41-I (DB 601A-1) inverted-vee-12; (205) 1,475hp Fiat RA1050 RC58 Tifone (Typhoon) (DB 605A-1).
Dimensions: Span 34ft 8½in (10·58m) (205N, 36ft 11in, 11·25m); length 29ft 0½in (8·85m) (205N, 31ft 4in, 9·55m); height 9ft 11½in (3·04m) (205N, 10ft 8in, 3·25m).
Weights: Empty (202) 5,181lb (2350kg), (205V) 5,691lb (2581kg), (205N-2) 6,082lb (2759kg); loaded (202) 6,636lb (3010kg), (205V) 7,514lb (3408kg), (205N-2) 8,364lb (3794kg).
Performance: Maximum speed (202) 370mph (595km/h), (205V) 399mph (642km/h), (205N-2) 389mph (626km/h); service ceiling (all) about 36,000ft (11,000m).
Armament: See text.
History: First flight (202) 10 August 1940; service delivery (202) July 1941; final delivery, early 1944.
User: Italy (RA, CB, ARSI).

Above: An M.C.202 Serie III. These were among the best fighters of the war, though available only in trivial numbers.

Above right: The prototype M.C.205V Veltro, first Italian fighter with the DB 605 engine, flown on 19 April 1942.

Right: Most of the handful of C.205V Veltro fighters served with the Aviazione Nazionale Repubblicana, the German puppet air force that continued to support the Axis after Italy's capitulation in October 1943. This Veltro is a Serie III aircraft with wing cannon serving instead with the Co-Belligerent air force.

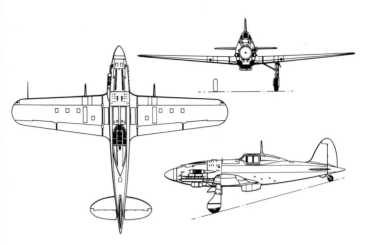

Above: Three-view of the Macchi C.205V Veltro.

Development: Essentially a re-engined Saetta, the MC202 was much more powerful and after quick and painless development went into production (first by Breda) in late 1940. Armament remained two 12·7mm Breda- ▶

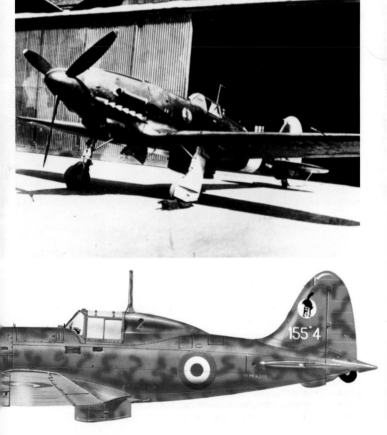

SAFAT above the engine and two 7·7mm Breda-SAFAT in the wings, plus two bombs up to 353lb (160kg) or tanks. From the outset the cockpit was completely enclosed, opposition to this having finally withered. Up to Serie VIII many aircraft had no wing guns, while at least one Serie had two 20mm Mauser MG 151/20 in underwing fairings. About 1,500 were built by 1943, 392 by Macchi, achieving complete superiority over the Hurricane and P-40. The more powerful 205 flew on 19 April 1942, but pathetic industrial performance (on engine as well as airframe) limited output to 262. The 205 Serie III dropped the 7·7mm wing guns in favour of MG 151/20s. The 205N was a total structural redesign instead of a converted 200, the first flying on 1 November 1942 with one MG 151/20 and four 12·7mm, two in the wing roots. It was an outstanding machine, retaining all the agility of earlier Macchi fighters, and the 205N-2 added powerful armament with two more MG 151/20 instead of the wing-root 12·7mm. None reached service.

Below: Folgores taxiing out for takeoff in 1943 prior to the Italian capitulation. This was the most important Italian aircraft in 1943, over 1,000 serving on Italian and Eastern Fronts.

Above: One of the C.205V Serie III Veltro fighters serving in 1944 with the ARSI (Aviazione Repubblica Sociale Italiana) which operated as one of the German satellite air forces.

Above: Wartime colour photograph of a Macchi C.202 Folgore taxiing out along a newly prepared taxiway. A ground-crewman rides on each wing, standard practice with poor-vision fighters.

Below: The C.202 Folgore was little more than a re-engined C.200. Despite the much longer and heavier engine manoeuvrability was almost as good as that of its predecessor, and critics of the four 12.7mm gun armament should note that this was the same as that of the P-51B Mustang.

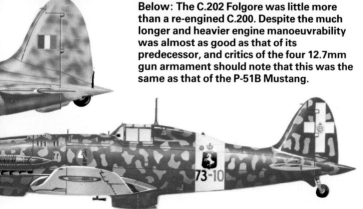

Reggiane Re 2000 series

Re 2000 Falco I (Falcon), 2001 Falco II, 2002 Ariete (Ram) and 2005 Sagittario (Archer)

Origin: Officine Meccaniche "Reggiane" SA; some Héjja built under licence by Mavag and Weiss Manfred, Hungary.
Type: Single-seat fighter.
Engine: (2000) one 1,025hp Piaggio P.XIbis RC40 14-cylinder two-row radial; (Héjja) 1,000hp WM K14; (2001) 1,175hp Alfa Romeo RA.1000 RC41 (DB 601) inverted-vee-12; (2002) 1,175hp Piaggio P.XIX RC45, (as P.XIbis); (2005) 1,475hp Fiat RA.1050 RC58 Tifone (Typhoon) (DB 605, as DB 601).
Dimensions: Span 36ft 1in (11m); length (2000) 26ft 2½in (7·95m); (2001–2) 26ft 10in; (2005) 28ft 7¾in; height (typical) 10ft 4in (3·15m).
Weight: Empty (2000) 4,200lb (1905kg); maximum loaded (2000) 5,722lb (2595kg); (2001) 7,231lb; (2002) 7,143lb; (2005) 7,848lb.
Performance: Maximum speed (2000–2) 329–337mph (say, 535km/h); (2005) 391mph (630km/h); initial climb (typical) 3,600ft (1100m)/min; service ceiling (2000) 36,745ft (11,200m); range (typical) 590 miles 950km).
Armament: See text.
History: First flight (2000) 1938; (2001) 1940; (2002) late 1941; (2005) September 1942. *continued* ▶

Right: This colourful fighter was a Héjja serving with Hungarian fighter squadron 1/1 on the Eastern Front in 1942. It was built in Italy in early 1940, but most Héjjas were constructed under licence in Hungary and were powered by a Wright R-1820 Cyclone or Manfred Weiss Gnome-Rhône K14 engine and had other detail differences.

Right: This Reggiane Re 2002 Ariete was one of a handful which reached the Regia Aeronautica prior to Italy's collapse in October 1943. So far as is known all went to the 5° Stormo da Assalto which was heavily engaged in Sicily and then southern Italy before being virtually eliminated. A handful also reached the 50° Stormo.

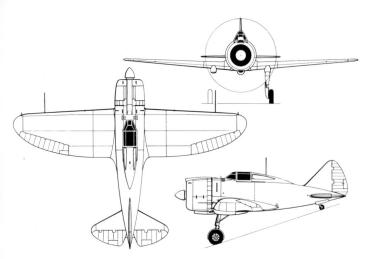

Above: Three-view of the Re 2000 Serie III.

Left: The 50° Stormo never became operational with the Re 2002 Ariete until after the capitulation in October 1943, and a handful of Arietes subsequently changed sides (as did this example) to fight with the Allied Co-Belligerent air force. This aircraft is depicted with an Italian 640kg (1,410lb) bomb, and tests were also made prior to the capitulation with a torpedo.

Users: (Re 2000) Hungary, Italy (Navy), Sweden; (2001) Italy (RA and ARSI); (2002) Germany (Luftwaffe), Italy (ARSI); (2005) Germany (Luftwaffe), Italy (ARSI).

Development: A subsidiary of Caproni, the Reggiane company copied the Seversky P-35 to produce the nimble but lightly built Re 2000. Extremely manoeuvrable, it had two 12·7mm Breda-SAFAT on the top decking and could carry a 441lb (200kg) bomb. Almost all the 170 built served non-Italian forces, Sweden using 60 (as the J 20) and Hungary about 100 (as the Héjja) on the Eastern front. Production of the 2001 reached 252, in four series with two 12·7mm either alone or augmented by two 7·7mm or (in 150 CN2 night fighters) 20mm wing guns, plus a 1,410lb (640kg) bomb. About 50 2002 were built and only 48 of the excellent 2005 with three 20mm and two 12·7mm.

Right: Only 252 Re 2001 Falco II fighters were completed, of which 150 were of the 2001 CN (Caccia Noce = night figher) version. The latter were painted black or blackish olive, but the Falco II shown here was a day fighter with the 362° Squadriglia, 22° Gruppo, Rome Capodichino, in May 1943. The 22° was named for ace Spauracchio.

Below: MM 494, the first prototype Re 2005 Sagittario, flown in September 1942. Only about 48 were delivered.

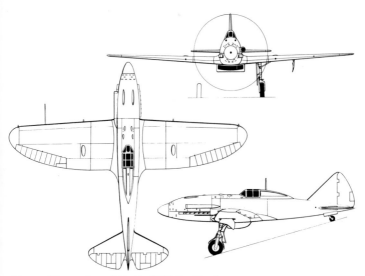

Above: Three-view of the Re 2005 Sagittario.

Left: It is claimed in Italian reports that, in mock dogfights against a Bf 109E in 1941 the Re 2000 Serie I was victorious in the hands of both Italian and German pilots. This fighter was however much too slow and weakly armed to be really effective.

Below: Reggiane Re 2001 CN night fighters, serving with the Regia Aeronautica before the armistice of September 1943.

JAPAN

As in the case of the Soviet Union, fighter development in Japan was almost completely unknown in Western countries at the time of Pearl Harbor in December 1941. For reasons never explained, the official belief in such places as London and Washington was that the Japanese could only make inferior copies of Western aircraft, and that their air force and navy was equipped almost entirely with biplanes with fixed landing gear – though there was abundant evidence to the contrary. The inevitable result was that when Allied pilots met Japanese fighters the latter were not merely a great and unpleasant shock but to some degree became regarded – on both sides – as almost invincible. Compared with the motley collection of second-rate Allied fighters, the Navy A6M and Army Ki-43 had adequate performance and just the essential superiority in manoeuvrability needed for victory, and especially in the case of the Navy fighter a range with drop tank greater than in any previous fighter enabled the Japanese to command the air at distances beyond anything Allied commanders had anticipated.

In fact the superiority of the Japanese fighters was only marginal, and magnified in practice by the immense psychological effect and the indifference of their opposition. In July 1942 an A6M was found almost undamaged but upside-down on an Aleutian island, and when it was dissected and test-flown in California it was found to be very far from invincible. In fact it was a typical 1937-style fighter, with only half the engine-power of the new crop of US fighters, and able to carry two wing cannon and a large quantity of fuel only by having a

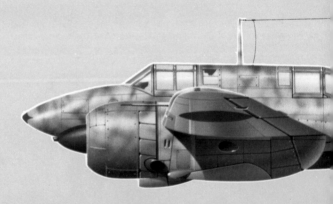

lightly built airframe and little protection It was clear that, as in Italy, a premium had been put on manoeuvrability at all costs.

Then the pendulum suddenly swung the other way; both Japanese Army and Navy staff officers and procurement officials decided their policy may have been mistaken and they bought fighters which sacrificed manoeuvrability and even pilot view to get more performance and firepower. Chief of this generation were the Army Ki-44 and Navy J2M, and the latter in particular was an outstanding fighter with excellent handling qualities. Like the Italians the Japanese seemed to have a knack for achieving good manoeuvrability with sweet handling, and in addition they had plenty of powerful engines including turbosupercharged types as good at high altitude as anything in the Allied nations. Yet the superior fighters suffered from delays and other problems, so that the ones the Allies met in numbers tended to be the same old A6M (Zero) and Ki-43 (Oscar).

One of the best Navy fighters was produced by the Kawanishi company by putting landing gear on a fighter seaplane; but it was complex and when a simplified model was developed and put into production on a gigantic scale the war was already nearly over. The Zero's direct replacement, the A7M, never did get into production. Radical new German-inspired jet and rocket fighters remained scarce prototypes without Germany's immense jet and rocket industrial background. Only one fighter introduced during World War II by Japan made any significant impact on the Allies, the Nakajima Ki-84 of the Army. And this, too, suffered from pinpricking snags that blunted its impact.

Aichi D3A "Val"

D3A1 and D3A2

Origin: Aichi Tokei Denki KK.
Type: Two-seat carrier dive bomber.
Engine: 1,075hp Mitsubishi Kinsei 44 14-cylinder radial (D3A2, 1,200hp Kinsei 54).
Dimensions: Span 47ft 1½in (14·365m); (D3A2) 47ft 8in (14·53m); length 33ft 5½in (10·2m); (D3A2) 33ft 7in (10·25m); height 11ft (3·35m); (D3A2 same).
Weights: Empty 5,309lb (2408kg); (D3A2) 5,772lb (2618kg); loaded 8,047lb (3650kg); (D3A2) 8,378lb (3800kg).
Performance: Maximum speed 242mph (389km/h); (D3A2) 281mph (450km/h); service ceiling 31,170ft (9500m); (D3A2) 35,700ft (10,880m); range with bomb 1,131 miles (1820km); (D3A2) 969 miles (1560km).
Armament: Two fixed 7·7mm guns in wings, one pivoted in rear cockpit; centreline bomb of 551lb (250kg), plus two bombs under wings each of 66lb (30kg); (D3A2: wing bombs 132lb, 60kg).
History: First flight August 1936; (D3A2) probably 1941; termination of production 1944.
User: Imperial Japanese Navy.

Development: In World War II the proper designations of Japanese aircraft were difficult to remember and often unknown to the Allies, so each major type was allotted a codename. Even today "Aichi D3A" may mean little to a grizzled veteran to whom the name "Val" will evoke memories of terrifying dive-bombing attacks. Aichi began this design for the Imperial Navy in 1936, its shape showing the influence of Heinkel who were secretly advising the Navy at that time. A total of 478 D3A1, also called Model 11 or Type 99, were built by August 1942, when production switched to the D3A2, Model 22. The D3A1 was the dive bomber that attacked Pearl Harbor on 7 December 1941. In April 1942 Aichis confirmed their bomb-hitting accuracy of 80–82% by sinking the British carrier *Hermes* and heavy cruisers *Cornwall* and *Dorsetshire*. They were extremely strong and manoeuvrable, and until 1943 were effective dogfighters after releasing their bombs. But loss of skilled pilots in great battles of 1943–44, especially

continued ▶

Right: Though inferior in several ways to the later and more numerous D3A2, it was the D3A1 that inflicted by far the gravest harm to the Allies. Skilfully flown by experienced crews, these aircraft devastated land targets and sank many ships including large surface combatants. Its design in the summer of 1936 was to some degree inspired by the Heinkel He 70, though the landing gear was fixed. The first production contract was placed in December 1939, and except for 201 of the later D3A2 model built by Showa at Tokyo all were made by Aichi at Nagoya.

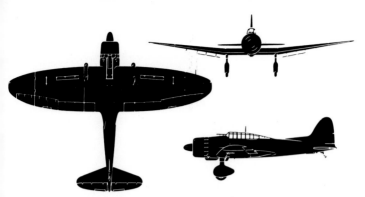

Above: Three-view of the cleaned-up Aichi D3A2.

Above; Takeoff of a D3A1 from a Japanese carrier on 7 December 1941, en route for Pearl Harbor and World War II.

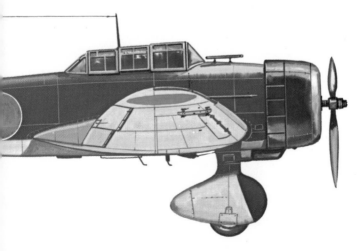

Above: A part of a scattered formation of the main production version, the D3A2 (Type 99 Model 22). Outward bound, these aircraft are carrying 250kg (551lb) bombs.

Right: In the final desperate months of the Pacific war hundreds of Japanese aircraft were used in one-way suicide missions. These D3A2s are leaving on such a mission from near Manila.

Midway and the Solomons, reduced bombing accuracy to 10% and the Aichis ceased to be the great threat they were in 1942. Production of the D3A2 was stopped in January 1944 at the 816th example of this cleaner and better-looking version. Some Aichis were converted as trainers or as overloaded Kamikaze aircraft. Nakajima developed a smaller version with retractable landing gear, the D3N1, but this was not adopted.

Aichi B7A Ryusei "Grace"

AM-23, 16-Shi Carrier Attack Bomber Ryusei (Shooting Star) (Allied code-name "Grace")

Origin: Aichi Kokuki KK; second-source production by Dai-Nijuichi Kaigun Kokusho (Sasebo Naval Air Arsenal).
Type: Two-seat carrier-based torpedo and dive bomber.
Engine: 1,825hp Nakajima NK9C Homare 12 18-cylinder radial.
Dimensions: Span 47ft 3in (14·40m); length 37ft 8½in (11·49m); height 13ft 4¼in (4·07m).
Weights: Empty 7,969lb (3614kg); loaded 12,568lb (5700kg).
Performance: Maximum speed 352mph (566km/h); service ceiling 29,365ft (8950m); range with full weapon load 1,150 miles (1850km); max range (overload) 1,889 miles (3040km).
Armament: Two 20mm Type 99 Model 2 in wings and single 7·92mm or 13mm gun aimed from rear cockpit; one 1,764lb (800kg) torpedo or similar weight of bombs.
History: First flight May 1942; service delivery May 1944; final delivery August 1945.
User: Japan (Imperial Navy).

Development: One of Japan's largest and most powerful carrier-based aircraft, the B7A was designed to a 1941 (16-Shi) specification for a fast and versatile aircraft to supplement and then replace the Nakajima B6N torpedo bomber and Yokosuka D4Y dive bomber. Though it did not carry

---

Kawanishi N1K1-J and 2-J Shiden "George"

N1K1-J and N1K2-J and variants

Origin: Kawanishi Kokuki KK; also built by Omura Kaigun Kokusho, Mitsubishi, Aichi, Showa and Dai-Juichi.
Type: Single-seat fighter.
Engine: One 1,990hp Nakajima Homare 21 18-cylinder two-row radial.
Dimensions: Span 39ft 3¼in (11·97m); length 29ft 1¾in (8·885m); (N1K2-J) 30ft 8½in (9·35m); height 13ft 3¾in (4·058m); (N1K2-J) 13ft (3·96m).
Weights: Empty 6,387lb (2897kg); (N1K2-J) 6,299lb (2657kg); maximum loaded 9,526lb (4321kg); (N1K2-J) 10,714lb (4860kg).
Performance: Maximum speed 362mph (583km/h); (N1K2-J) 369mph (594km/h); initial climb (both) 3,300ft (1000m)/min; service ceiling 39,698ft (12,100m); (N1K2-J) 35,400ft (10,760m); range 989 miles (1430km); (N1K2-J) 1,069 miles (1720km).
Armament: Originally two 20mm in wings and two 7·7mm above fuselage; after 20 aircraft, two extra 20mm added in underwing blisters; (N1K1-Ja) as before without 7·7mm; N1K2-J, four 20mm in pairs inside wing, with more ammunition, plus two 550lb (250kg) bombs underwing or six rockets under fuselage; later prototypes, heavier armament.
History: First flight 24 July 1943; first flight (N1K2-J) 3 April 1944.
User: Japan (Imperial Navy).

Above: A rare photograph of a fully operational B7A, complete with torpedo, apparently about to depart on a combat mission. Every operational flight was from land airstrips.

any more weapons than its predecessors, the B7A1 prototype proved to be greatly superior in performance, with speed and manoeuvrability at least as good as an A6M "Zero". Unfortunately the troublesome engine delayed development until Japan had lost command of the air, and by the time deliveries took place the last carriers were being sunk and home industry bombed to a standstill (the destruction of the Aichi Funakata plant by a May 1945 earthquake did not help). Only 114 aircraft flew, nine being B7A1 prototypes and the rest B7A2 production machines used from land bases.

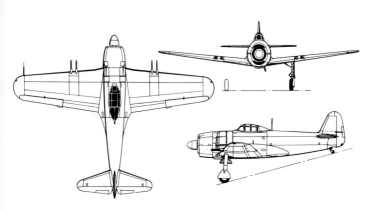

Above: three-view of N1K2-J Shiden-Kai.

Development: In September 1940 the JNAF issued a requirement for a high-speed seaplane naval fighter that did not need land airfields but could maintain air superiority during island invasions. The result was the formidable N1K1 Kyofu (mighty wind), produced by Kawanishi's Naruo plant and code-named "Rex" by the Allies. It was from this central-float seaplane that Kikuhara's team very quickly devised the N1K1-J landplane (Allied name: "George"). Though a hasty lash-up it was potentially one of the best of all Japanese fighters. Its manoeuvrability, boosted by automatic combat flaps worked by a manometer (mercury U-tube) that measured angle of attack, was almost unbelievable. Drawbacks were the engine, ▶

Above: The N1K2-J had 23,000 fewer parts than the complex original version, but it appeared too late to influence the war.

plagued with snags, the poor view with the mid wing and the complex and weak landing gear (legacy from the mid-wing float-plane and big four-blade propeller). Naruo therefore produced the N1K2-J with low wing, new tail and drastically simpler airframe that could be built in half the man-hours.

Kawasaki Ki-45 Toryu "Nick"
Ki-45 and 45A, Heavy Fighter Type 2, Kai B, C and D

Origin: Kawasaki Kokuki Kogyo.
Type: Originally long-range escort; later night fighter and attack.
Engines: Two 1,080hp Mitsubishi Ha-102 (Type 1) 14-cylinder two-row radials.
Dimensions: Span 49ft 3½in (15·02m); length (Kai C) 36ft 1in (11m); height 12ft 1½in (3·7m).
Weights: Empty (Kai A) 8,340lb (3790kg); (Kai C) 8,820lb (4000kg); loaded (all) 12,125lb (5500kg).
Performance: Maximum speed (all) 336mph (540km/h); initial climb 2,300ft (700m)/min; service ceiling 32,800ft (10,000m); range, widely conflicting reports, but best Japanese sources suggest 1,243 miles (2000km) with combat load for all versions.

continued ▶

The unreliable engine still kept Shidens (the name meant violet lightning) mostly unserviceable, but they were potent and respected adversaries, encountered on all fronts from May 1944. Total production was 1,440. Huge production was planned from four companies and four Navy arsenals, but none produced more than ten aircraft, other than Kawanishi which delivered 543 1-Js and 362 2-Js from Naruo and 468 1-Js and 44 2-Js from Himeji. At Okinawa both versions were used in the Kamikaze role.

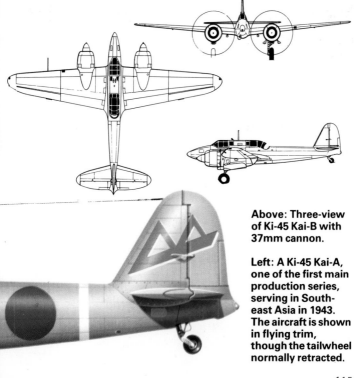

Above: Three-view of Ki-45 Kai-B with 37mm cannon.

Left: A Ki-45 Kai-A, one of the first main production series, serving in South-east Asia in 1943. The aircraft is shown in flying trim, though the tailwheel normally retracted.

Armament: (Ki-45-I and Kai-A) two 12·7mm fixed in nose and two 7·7 mm manually aimed from rear cockpit; (Kai-B) same plus 37mm cannon in lower right forward fuselage (often with only one 12·7mm); (Kai-C) adapted for night fighting in May 1944, two 12·7mm installed at 30° between cockpits, with two 12·7mm and one 20mm or 37mm in nose; antiship versions, said to have carried 50mm or 75mm gun under nose, plus two 551lb (250kg) bombs under wings.

History: First flight (Ha-20 engine) January 1939; (Ha-25 engine) July 1940; (production Ki-45) September 1941.

User: Japan (Imperial Army).

Development: The first twin-engined fighter of the Imperial Japanese Army, the Ki-45 Toryu (dragon-slayer) was a long time in gestation. It was designed at Kawasaki's Gifu factory to meet a 1936 requirement issued in March 1937. Kawasaki had never used twin air-cooled engines and the

Top of page: Two pre-production development Ki-45s, probably photographed in 1942. Both differ from early production Ki-45s.

Nakajima Ha-20B was an undeveloped engine which misbehaved; pilots disliked the hand-cranked landing gear. After trying contraprops, the choice fell on the Navy Ha-25 Sakae engine, but this in turn was replaced by the Ha-102 soon after production began in 1941. The Akashi plant began to build the Ki-45 as a second source in late 1942, but combined output was only 1,698. Despite this modest total, and the fact that these aircraft were continually being modified, they were met on every Pacific front and known as "Nick". They were fairly fast and manoeuvrable but not really formidable until, on 27 May 1944, four Kai-B (modification B) made the first-ever suicide attack (on the north coast of New Guinea). By mid-1944 most Ki-45s had been modified to Kai-C configuration as night fighters, claiming seven victories over B-29s on the night of 15 June 1944. The two main Ki-45 bases at the close of the war were Hanoi and Anshan (Manchuria), from which aircraft made night interceptions and day Kamikaze attacks. The Ki-45 never operated in its design role of long-range escort.

Left: This colourful Ki-45 was a Hei (Kai-C) of the 53rd Sentai based at Matsudo, Chiba Prefecture. Assigned to the Shinten unit, its mission was interception of B-29s in mid-1945

Below: The first prototype differed markedly from later Ki-45s and, like the second, had elliptical wings and Ha-20b (Bristol Mercury) engines.

Kawasaki Ki-61 Hien "Tony"

Ki-61-I, II and III (Type 3 fighter) and Ki-100 (Type 5)

Origin: Kawasaki Kokuki Kogyo.

Type: Single-seat fighter.

Engine: (Ki-61-I) one 1,175hp Kawasaki Ha-40 inverted-vee 12 liquid-cooled; (Ki-61-II) one 1,450hp Kawasaki Ha-140 of same layout; (Ki-100) one 1,500hp Mitsubishi Ha-112-II 14-cylinder two-row radial.

Dimensions: Span 39ft 4½in (12m); length (-I) 29ft 4in (8·94m); (-II) 30ft 0½in (9·16m); (Ki-100) 28ft 11¼in (8·82m); height (all) 12ft 2in (3·7m).

Weights: Empty (-I) 5,798lb (2630kg); (-II) 6,294lb (2855kg); (Ki-100) 5,567lb (2525kg); loaded (-I) 7,650lb (3470kg); (-II) 8,433lb (3825kg); (Ki-100) 7,705lb (3495kg).

Performance: Maximum speed (-I) 348mph (560km/h); (-II) 379mph (610km/h); (Ki-100) 367mph (590km/h); initial climb (-I, -II) 2,200ft (675m)/min; (Ki-100) 3,280ft (1000m)/min; service ceiling (-I) 32,800ft (10,000m); (-II) 36,089ft (11,000m); (Ki-100) 37,729ft (11,500m); range (-I, -II) 990–1,100 miles (-I, 1800km, -II, 1600km); (Ki-100) 1,243 miles (2000km).

Armament: (Ki-61-Ia) two 20mm MG 151/20 in wings, two 7·7mm above engine; (-Id) same but wing guns 30mm; (-IIb) four 20mm Ho-5 in wings; (Ki-100) two Ho-5 in wings and two 12·7mm in fuselage, plus underwing racks for two 551lb (250kg) bombs.

History: First flight (Ki-60) March 1941; (Ki-61) December 1941; service delivery (Ki-61-I) August 1942; first flight (-II) August 1943; (Ki-100) 1 February 1945.

User: Japan (Imperial Army).

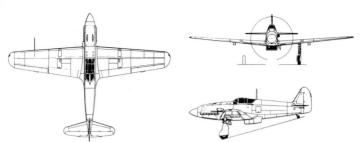

Above: Three-view of Ki-61 (interim aircraft with canopy having features of -I and -II and wing of -IIa).

Development: Kawasaki purchased a licence to build the German DB 601 engine in 1937 and the resulting revised and lightened engine emerged in 1940 as the Ha-40. Around this engine Kawasaki planned the Ki-60 and a lighter fighter designated Ki-61. Hien (the Japanese name meaning flying swallow). The latter was completed in December 1941 and flew well, reaching a speed of 368mph. During the first half of 1942 the prototype was extensively tested, performing very well against a captured P-40E and a Bf 109E sent to Japan by submarine. The submarine also brought 800 Mauser MG 151 cannon, and these were fitted to most early Ki-61s despite the unreliability of the supply of electrically fired ammunition. The Gifu plant delivered 2,654 (according to one authority, 2,750) Ki-61-I and -Ia, the latter being redesigned for easier servicing and increased manoeuvrability. They went into action around New Guinea in April 1943, were called "Tony" by the Allies, and were the only Japanese fighters with a liquid-cooled ▶

Below: One of the first Ki-61s, probably built about the time of Pearl Harbor, with Ha-40 engine and original style of canopy. It was evaluated successfully against many other fighters.

engine. They were constantly in air combat, later moving to the Philippines and finally back to Japan. By 1944 the Ki-61-II was trickling off the assembly line with an unreliable engine that could not meet production demands. The II had a bigger wing and new canopy, but was soon replaced by the IIa with the old, proven, wing. Only 374 of all -II versions were built, and in early 1945 one of 275 engineless airframes was fitted with the Ha-112 radial.

Kawasaki Ki-102 "Randy"

Ki-102a, b and c
(Allied code-name "Randy")

Origin: Kawasaki Kokuki Kogyo KK.
Type: Two-seat (a) high-altitude fighter, (b) ground-attack aircraft or (c) night fighter.
Engines: Two 1,500hp Mitsubishi Ha-112 14-cylinder radials, (a, c) Ha-112-II Ru with turbochargers.
Dimensions: Span (a, b) 51ft 1in (15·57m), (c) 56ft 6¼in (17·23m); length (a, b) 37ft 6¾in (11·45m), (c) 42ft 9¾in (13·05m); height 12ft 1¾in (3·70m).
Weights: Empty (a) 11,354lb (5150kg), (b) 10,913lb (4950kg), (c) 11,464lb (5200kg); loaded (a) 15,763lb (7150kg), (b) 16,094lb (7300kg), (c) 16,755lb (7600kg).
Performance: Maximum speed (a, b) 360mph (580km/h), (c) 373mph (600km/h); service ceiling (a) 42,650ft (13,000m), (b) 32,800ft (10,000m), (c) 44,295ft (13,500m); range (a, b) 1,243 miles (2000km), (c) 1,367 miles (2200km).
Armament: (a) one fixed 37mm Ho-203 in nose and two 20mm Ho-5 below, (b) one 57mm Ho-401 in nose, two Ho-5 below and manually aimed 12·7mm Ho-103 in rear cockpit, (c) two 30mm Ho-105 under fuselage and two 20mm Ho-5 mounted obliquely.
History: First flight March 1944; service delivery, about November 1944.
User: Japan (Imperial Army).

Development: In August 1942 the Ki-45 Toryu design team under

Left: Many Japanese fighters, of both the Imperial Army and Navy, were colourful. This Ki-61-IIb was assigned to the 244th Sentai of the 2nd Chutai, based in the Tokyo Defence Area in 1945 attempting to intercept high-flying B-29s and, at the end of the war, also having to tangle with the P-51D Mustang which was distinctly superior. The IIb(II Kai-B) did, however, have greater firepower with four Ho-5 cannon of 20mm calibre.

Despite the sudden lash-up conversion the result was a staggeringly fine fighter, easily the best ever produced in Japan. With desperate haste this conversion went into production as the Ki-100. One of the first Ki-100 units destroyed 14 Hellcats without loss to themselves in their first major battle over Okinawa and this easily flown and serviced machine fought supremely well against B-29s and Allied fighters to the end.

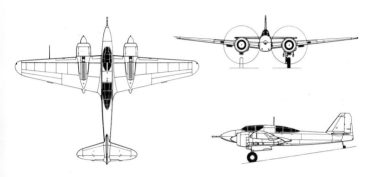

Above: Ki-102b with long-barrel 57mm and without D/F acorn.

Takeo Doi began work on a development designated Ki-96, three of these 3,000hp single-seat "heavy fighters" being built. In August 1943 approval was given for a further development with crew of two for use in the ground-attack role. Three prototypes and 20 pre-production Ki-102 were built, followed by 215 Ki-102b (Ki-102 Otsu) of which a few saw action in Okinawa. Some were used in the Igo-1-B air-to-ground missile programme. Two were rebuilt with pressure cabin as prototypes of the Ki-108, but the size of development task for this led to the Ki-102a being launched as a high-altitude fighter without pressure cabin. About 15 were delivered in July-August 1945 as the Ki-102 Ko. Right at the end of the war two Ki-102b were completely rebuilt as prototypes of the 102c night fighter with AI radar, greater span and length, new cockpit with rear-facing radar operator and different armament.

Left: An apparently standard Ki-102b after capture in 1945. In the nose is the muzzle of the short-barrel 57mm gun and a D/F loop acorn is visible above the mid-fuselage. Little known until after the war, Ki-102 was a useful type.

Mitsubishi A5M "Claude"

A5M1 to A5M4

Origin: Mitsubishi Jukogyo KK; also built by Dai-Nijuichi KK and KK Watanabe Tekkosho.

Type: Single-seat carrier-based fighter.

Engine: One Nakajima Kotobuki (Jupiter) nine-cylinder radial; (1) 585hp 2-Kai-I; (2) 610hp 2-Kai-3; (4) 710hp Kotobuki 41 or (A5M4 Model 34) 3-Kai.

Dimensions: Span (2) 35ft 6in, (4) 36ft 1in (11·0m); length (2) 25ft 7in; (4) 24ft 9½in (7·55m); height 10ft 6in (3·2m).

Weights: Empty (2, typical) 2,400lb (1090kg); (4) 2,681lb (1216kg); maximum loaded (2) 3,545lb (1608kg); (4) 3,763lb (1708kg).

Performance: Maximum speed (2) 265mph (426km/h); (4) 273mph (440km/h); initial climb (2) 2,215ft (675m)/min; (4) 2,790ft (850m)/min; service ceiling (typical, all) 32,800ft (10,000m); range (2) 460 miles (740km); (4, auxiliary tank) 746 miles (1200km).

Armament: (All) two 7·7mm Type 89 machine guns firing on each side of upper cylinder of engine; racks for two 66lb (30kg) bombs under outer wings.

History: First flight 4 February 1935; service delivery 1936; final delivery December 1939.

User: Japan (Imperial Navy).

Development: One of the neatest little warplanes of its day, the A5M was the chief fighter of the Imperial Japanese Navy throughout the Sino-Japanese war and was numerically the most important at the time of Pearl Harbor. It was built to meet a 1934 specification calling for a speed of 218mph and ability to reach 16,400ft in 6½ minutes, and beat these figures by a wide margin. Within days of first flight at Kagamigahara the Ka-14 prototype exceeded 279mph and reached 16,400ft in 5min 54sec, which the Japanese considered "far above the world level at that time". It was the Navy's first

Right: Two A5M2 fighters (they are probably 2a models) of a training unit photographed in the late 1930s. This model had a two-blade propeller but was otherwise very like the most important version, the long-range A5M4. The aircraft nearest the camera has had its rear spat sections removed.

Below: Probably photographed over China in about 1937, these appear to be of the original A5M1 version. Fuselage slogans were not uncommon.

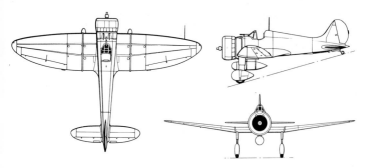

Above: Three-view of A5M4 with long-range tank.

monoplane fighter, and one of the first all-metal stressed-skin machines built in Japan. The production A5M1, called Type 96 or S-96 and later given the Allied code name "Claude", abandoned the prototype's inverted-gull wing, originally chosen to try to improve pilot view, and also switched to a direct drive engine. The elliptical wing had split flaps, manoeuvrablity was superb and from their first combat mission on 18 September 1937, with the 2nd Combined Air Flotilla based at Shanghai, they acquitted themselves very well. During the conflict with the Soviet Union along the Manchukuo-Mongolian border throughout 1939 the A5M proved the biggest menace to the Russian aircraft, having earlier, on 2 December 1937, destroyed no fewer than ten I-16Bs of the Chinese in one dogfight over Nanking. Such results completely overcame the Naval pilots' earlier distrust of so speedy a monoplane and when the final A5M4 model entered service it was very popular. Mitsubishi built "about 800" (one source states 782), while Kyushu Aircraft (Watanabe) and the Sasebo naval dockyard (D-N) made 200 more. The final version was the A5M4-K dual trainer produced by conversion of fighters in 1941.

Mitsubishi A6M Zero-Sen "Zeke"

A6M1 to A6M8c and Nakajima A6M2-N

Origin: Mitsubishi Jukogyo KK; also built by Nakajima Hikoki KK.

Type: Single-seat carrier-based fighter, (A6M2-N) float seaplane.

Engine: (A6M1) one 780hp Mitsubishi MK2 Zuisei 13 14-cylinder two-row radial: (M2) 925hp Nakajima NK1C Sakae 12 of same layout; (M3) 1,130hp Sakae 21; (M5) as M3 with individual exhaust stacks; (M6c) Sakae 31 with same rated power but water/methanol boost to 1,210hp for emergency; (M8c) 1,560hp Mitsubishi Kinsei 62 of same layout.

Dimensions: Span (1, 2) 39ft 4½in (12·0m); (remainder) 36ft 1in (11·0m); length (all landplanes) 29ft 9in (9·06m); (A6M2-N) 33ft 2¾in (10·13m); height (1, 2) 9ft 7in (2·92m); (all later landplanes) 9ft 8in (2·98m); (A6M2-N) 14ft 1½in (4·3m).

Weights: Empty (2) 3,704lb (1680kg); (3) 3,984lb (1807kg); (5) typically 3,920lb (1778kg); (6c) 4,175lb (1894kg); (8c) 4,740lb (2150kg); (A6M2-N) 3,968lb (1800kg); maximum loaded (2) 5,313lb (2410kg); (3) 5,828lb (2644kg); (5c) 6,050lb (2733kg; 2952kg as overload); (6c) as 5c; (8c) 6,944lb (3149kg); (A6M2-N) 5,423lb (2460kg).

Performance: Maximum speed (2) 316mph (509km/h); (3) 336mph (541km/h); (5c, 6c) 354mph (570km/h); (8c) 360mph (580km/h); (A6M2-N) 273mph (440km/h); initial climb (1, 2, 3) 4,500ft (1370m)/min; (5, 6c) 3,150ft (960m)/min; (2-N) not known; service ceiling (1, 2) 33,790ft (10,300m); (3) 36,250ft (11,050m); (5c, 6c) 37,500ft (11,500m); (8c) 39,370ft (12,000m); (A6M2-N) 32,800ft (10,000m); range with drop tank (2) 1,940 miles (3110km); (5) 1,200 miles (1920km).

Armament: (1, 2, 3 and 2-N) two 20mm Type 99 cannon each with 60-round drum fixed in outer wings, two 7·7mm Type 97 machine guns each with 500 rounds above front fuselage, and wing racks for two 66lb (30kg) bombs; (5a) two 20mm Type 99 Mk 4 with belt of 85 rounds per gun, two 7·7mm in fuselage and wing racks for two 132lb (60kg) bombs; (5b) as 5a but one 7·7mm replaced by 12·7mm; (5c and all later versions) two 20mm Type 99 Mk 4 and two 13·2mm in wings, one 13·2mm (optional) in fuselage, plus wing racks for two 60kg.

History: First flight 1 April 1939; service delivery (A6M1) late July 1940; first flight (A6M2-N) December 1941; (A6M5) August 1943; (A6M2-K) January 1942.

User: Japan (Imperial Navy).

continued ▶

Right: One of the later versions of Japan's most important combat aircraft was the A6M5 Model 52, with stronger non-folding wings and various detail changes including ejector-stack exhausts. This example served with the Gensan Kokutai at Wonsan (Korea) in December 1944.

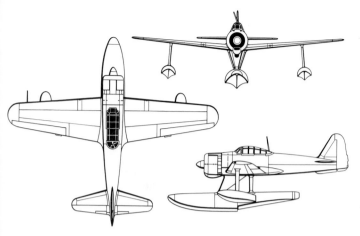

Above: Three-view of A6M2-N, by Nakajima.

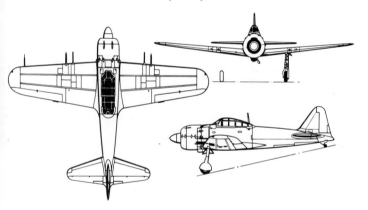

Above: Three-view of A6M5c, which introduced the final armament but was severely underpowered with unboosted engine.

Left: Painted sky grey overall, and with the markings of the *Hiryu* (aircraft carrier) group (2nd Koku Sentai) at the time of Pearl Harbor, this A6M2 was one of the first Japanese fighters to participate in World War II. It is almost beyond belief that the Allies had no knowledge of this fighter, used for years in China against US Army pilots and forming two-thirds of Navy seagoing fighter strength.

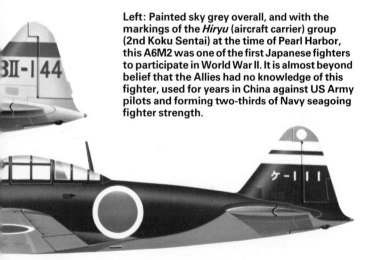

Development: The most famous of all Japanese combat aircraft possessed the unique distinction of being the first carrier-based fighter ever to out-perform corresponding land-based machines; it was also a singularly unpleasant shock to US and British staff which had apparently never studied the behaviour of this fighter in China or even discovered its existence. It was designed by Mitsubishi to meet the severe demands of the 1937 Navy carrier-based fighter specification, seeking a successor to the A5M. Demands included a speed of 500km/h (311mph) and armament of two cannon and two machine guns. Under team leader Jiro Horikoshi the new fighter took shape as a clean, efficient but lightly built aircraft with out-standing manoeuvrability. With a more powerful engine it was accepted for production as the A6M2, though as it was put into production in 1940, the Japanese year 5700, it became popularly the Zero-Sen (Type 00 fighter), and to millions of its enemies was simply the "Zero" (though the official Allied code name was "Zeke"). Before official trials were completed two squadrons with 15 aircraft were sent to China in July 1940 for trials under operational conditions. They eliminated all opposition, as forcefully reported to Washington by Gen Claire Chennault, commander of the Flying Tigers volunteer force (his warning was obviously filed before being read). More than 400 had been delivered by the time the A6M2 and clipped-wing M3 appeared at Pearl Harbor. During the subsequent year it seemed that thousands of these fighters were in use, their unrivalled manoeuvrability being matched by unparalleled range with a small engine, 156gal internal fuel and drop tanks. So completely did the A6M sweep away Allied air power that the Japanese nation came to believe it was invincible. After the Battle of Midway the Allies slowly gained the ascendancy, and the A6M found itself outclassed by the F4U and F6F. Mitsubishi urgently tried to devise improved versions and the A6M5 was built in quantities far ▶

Above: One of the best photographs of the Zero-Sen in service, this 1942 picture shows A6M3 Model 22 fighters, the first subtype to have the full wingspan restored with fixed rounded tips. These Zeros belonged to the 251st Kokutai and typified the long-range aircraft which during the Guadalcanal campaign operated up to 650 miles from their home bases.

Below: Nakajima developed the A6M2-N float seaplane version, and delivered the production batch of 327. They saw much action but were unable to win many combats against Allied fighters.

greater than any other Japanese combat aircraft. Improvements were mainly small and the combat-boosted Sakae 31 engine did not appear until the end of 1944. Only a few of the much more powerful A6M8c type were produced, the main reason for this change of engine being destruction of the Nakajima factory. The final model was the A6M7 Kamikaze version, though hundreds of Zeros of many sub-types were converted for suicide attacks. Total production amounted to 10,937, of which 6,217 were built by Nakajima which also designed and built 327 of the attractive A6M2-N single-float seaplane fighter version (code name "Rufe") which operated throughout the Pacific war. The A6M2-K was one of several dual trainer versions.

Right: Nearly all the identifiable Zeros in this photograph are of the A6M5 Model 52 version, the most numerous of all. The picture probably dates from 1943, when this once outstanding fighter was due to have been supplanted in production by the A7M Reppu. Complete failure to produce the new aircraft resulted in prolonged A6M5 production. The same thing happened to many front-line types for the Luftwaffe such as the Ju 87, He 111 and Bf 110.

Below: A frame from a propaganda ciné film taken on board the aircraft carrier *Hiryu* at the start of the Pearl Harbor raid just after dawn on 7 December 1941. The A6M2 in the foreground heads a close mass of B5N torpedo bombers. The ship had 18 of each type, as well as 18 D3As.

Mitsubishi J2M Raiden "Jack"

J2M1 to J2M7

Origin: Mitsubishi Jukogyo KK; also small number (J2M5) built by Koza Kaigun Kokusho.

Type: Single-seat Navy land-based interceptor.

Engine: Most versions, one 1,820hp Mitsubishi MK4R-A Kasei 23a 14-cylinder two-row radial; (J2M5) 1,820hp MK4U-A Kasei 26a.

Dimensions: Span 35ft 5$\frac{1}{4}$in (10·8m); length (most) 31ft 9$\frac{3}{8}$in (9·70m); (J2M5) 32ft 7$\frac{3}{4}$in (9·95m); height (most) 12ft 6in (3·81m); (J2M5) 12ft 11$\frac{1}{4}$in (3·94m).

Weights: Empty (2) 5,572lb (2527kg); (3) 5,675lb (2574kg); (5) 6,259lb (2839kg); normal loaded (2) 7,257lb (3300kg); (3) 7,573lb (3435kg); (5) 7,676lb (3482kg); max overload (2, 3) 8,700lb (3946kg).

Performance: Maximum speed (2) 371mph (596km/h); (3) 380mph (612km/h); (5) 382mph (615km/h); initial climb (2, 3) 3,610ft (1100m)/min; (5) 3,030ft (925m)/min; range (2, 3 at normal gross) 655 miles (1055km); (2, 3 overload) 1,580 miles (2520km); (5, normal gross with 30min reserve) 345 miles (555km).

Armament: See text.

History: First flight (prototype) 20 March 1942; service delivery (J2M2) December 1943; first flight (J2M5) May 1944.

User: Japan (Imperial Navy).

Development: Though designed by a team led by the legendary Jiro Horikoshi, creator of the Zero-Sen, this utterly different little interceptor did little to enhance reputations, though there was nothing fundamentally faulty in its conception. It broke totally new ground, partly in being an interceptor for the Navy (previously the preserve of the Army) and partly in the reversal of design parameters. Instead of concentrating on combat manoeuvrability at all costs the J1M was designed solely for speed and fast climb. Manoeuvrability and even handling took second place. Unusual features in the basic design included a tiny laminar-flow wing fitted with combat flaps, a finely streamlined engine with propeller extension shaft and fan cooling, a very shallow enclosed canopy and a surprising number of forged parts in the stressed-skin airframe. Powered by a 1,460hp Kasei, the prototype Mitsubishi M-20, named Raiden (Thunderbolt), gave a great deal of trouble and was almost redesigned to produce the J2M2 with different engine, much deeper canopy, multi-stack exhaust and new four-blade propeller. Even then the Raiden suffered endless snags and crashes,

Below: Representing a complete break with all previous tradition in Japanese fighter design, the J2M was tailored to performance rather than pilot view and manoeuvrability. This J2M3 Raiden 21a of the 302nd Kokutai had the heavy armament of four of the new fast-firing Type 99-II cannon. The planned output of 500 a month wasn't even approached.

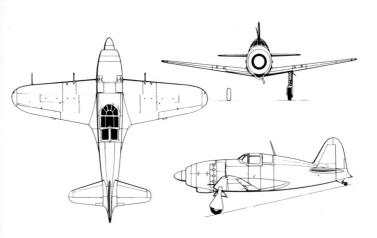

Above: Three-view of J2M3.

Above: One of the first J2M3 Raiden Type 21 fighters, the first model to have four cannon. At first the latter were all of the Type I variety but these were gradually replaced by Type II.

but eventually 155 J2M2 were delivered with two 20mm Type 99 and two 7·7mm above the fuselage. Production then switched to the J2M3 with machine guns removed and the wing fitted with two Type 99 and two fast-firing Type 99-II. The J2M3a had four Type 99-II. Fitted with bulged canopy these models became the J2M6 and 6a. A few high-flying J2M4 turbocharged versions were built, with six cannon, the two added guns being in the top fuselage decking. Best of all was the J2M5 with only two (wing) cannon but a far better engine, and it proved formidable against high-flying B-29s. After VJ-day, when only 480 of all models had been built by Mitsubishi (one month's planned output!), the Allies (who called this fighter "Jack") spoke in glowing terms of its performance and handling.

Mitsubishi Ki-15 "Babs"

Ki-15-I, Ki-15-II, C5M, Karigane

Origin: Mitsubishi Jukogyo KK.
Type: Two-seat light attack bomber.
Engine: (I) one 750hp Nakajima Ha-8 nine-cylinder radial; (II) one 800hp Mitsubishi A.14 (later named Kinsei) 14-cylinder two-row radial.
Dimensions: Span 39ft 4¾in (12·0m); length (I) 27ft 11in (8·50m); height 9ft 10in (3·0m).
Weights: Empty (I) 3,968lb (1800kg); maximum loaded (I) 5,070lb (2300kg); (II) 6,834lb (3100kg).
Performance: Maximum speed (I) 280mph (450km/h); (II) about 298mph (480km/h); initial climb (both) about 1,640ft (500m)/min; service ceiling (I) 28,220ft (8600m); range with bomb load (both) about 1,100 miles (1800km).
Armament: One 7·7mm Type 89 (not always fitted) fixed in outer wing firing forward, and one manually aimed from rear cockpit; bomb load of up to 551lb (250kg) in (I) or 1,100lb (500kg) in (II) carried externally.
History: First flight (Karigane prototype) May 1936; (Ki-15-I) probably late 1936.
User: Imperial Japanese Army.

Development: This trim little machine stemmed from a private venture by the giant Mitsubishi company, inspired by the emergence in the United States of modern stressed-skin monoplanes (particularly the Northrop A-17). With company funds, but sponsored by the Asahi (Rising Sun) newspaper, a prototype was built to demonstrate the ability of the fast-growing Japanese industry to build modern aircraft. It was a time of intense nationalism and the resulting machine, named Karigane (Wild Goose) by Mitsubishi, was individually christened "Kamikaze" (Divine Wind) and prepared as an instrument of national publicity. Its greatest achievement was a notably trouble-free flight of 9,900 miles from Tokyo to London in April 1937. Others were built for similar purposes (one being "Asakaze" (Morning Wind) of the Asahi Press) and as fast mailplanes, while in 1938 a small batch was built with the 550hp Kotobuki (licence-built Bristol Jupiter) replaced by the much more powerful A.14 engine. In 1937 construction began of 437 military Ki-15 series for the Army and these were soon one of the first really modern types to go into action in the Sino-Japanese war, which had simmered for years and finally broke out in 1937. The Ki-15 was used for level bombing, close support and photo-reconnaissance, but was replaced by the Ki-30 (p. 156). In 1939 the Imperial Navy began to receive 50 of two C5M versions with different engines. Allied code name was "Babs".

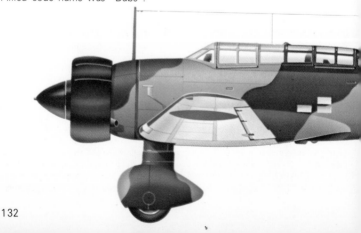

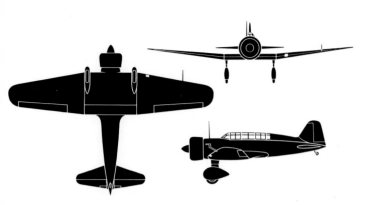

Above: Three-view of Mitsubishi Ki-15-I.

Above: Ki-15-I reconnaissance aircraft serving as pilot/observer trainers at the Kumagaya flying school (note badge on rudder).

Left: A Mitsubishi Ki-15-I of the 1st Chutai, 15th Hikosentai, of the Imperial Army. When the second Sino-Japanese war broke out in 1937 the Ki-15 was one of the first types to go into action. It had a speed higher than that of any Chinese aircraft except the Soviet-supplied I-16. It was a C5M2 of the Navy's 22nd Koku Sentai that, on 10 December 1941, spotted the warships HMS *Prince of Wales* and *Repulse;* a few hours later land-based bombers had sent both ships to the bottom.

Mitsubishi Ki-46 "Dinah"

Type 100 Models 1-4 (Ki-46-I to Ki-46-IVb)

Origin: Mitsubishi Jukogyo KK.
Type: Strategic reconnaissance (Ki-46-III-Kai, night fighter).
Engines: (I) two 870hp Mitsubishi Ha-26-I 14-cylinder two-row radials; (II) two 1,080hp Mitsubishi Ha-102 of same layout; (III) two 1,500hp Mitsubishi Ha-112-II of same layout; (IV) Ha-112-IIRu, same rated power but turbocharged.
Dimensions: Span 48ft $2\frac{3}{4}$in (14·7m); length (all except III-Kai) 36ft 1in (11·0m); (III-Kai) 37ft 8in (11·47m); height 12ft $8\frac{3}{4}$in (3·88m).
Weights: Empty (I) 7,450lb (3379kg); (II) 7,193lb (3263kg); (III) 8,446lb (3831kg); (IV) 8,840lb (4010kg); loaded (no overload permitted) (I) 10,630lb (4822kg); (II) 11,133lb (5050kg); (III) 12,620lb (5724kg); (IV) 13,007lb (5900kg); (III-Kai) 13,730lb (6227kg).
Performance: Maximum speed (I) 336mph (540km/h); (II) 375mph (604km/h); (III, III-Kai, IV) 391mph (630km/h); initial climb (I, II, III) about 1,970ft (600m)/min; (IV) 2,625ft (800m)/min; service ceiling (I, II, III) 34,500–36,000ft (10,500–11,000m); (IV) 38,000ft (11,500m); range (I) 1,305 miles (2100km); (II) 1,490 miles (2400km); (III) 2,485 miles (4000km); (III-Kai) 1,243 miles (2000km); (IV) not known, but at least 4000km.
Armament: (I, II) one 7·7mm manually aimed from rear cockpit; other types, none, except III-Kai, two 20mm Ho-5 cannon fixed in nose firing ahead and 37mm Ho-203 firing at elevation of 30° from top of fuselage.
History: First flight November 1939; (production II) March 1941; (III) December 1942; (III-Kai conversion) about September 1944.
User: Japan (Imperial Army).

Development: One of the most trouble-free and popular aircraft of the whole Pacific war, the Ki-46 "Shitei" (reconnaissance for HQ), code-named "Dinah" by the Allies, was one of only very few Japanese aircraft that could penetrate Allied airspace with some assurance it would survive. It was also almost the only machine with the proven ability to operate at the flight levels of the B-29. In the first year of its use, which extended to every part of the Japanese war throughout the Pacific and China, much trouble was experienced from sparking-plug erosion and crew anoxia, both rectified by improved design and greater oxygen storage. Allied radar forced the Ki-46 to fly even faster and higher, leading to the almost perfectly streamlined ▶

Right: Parachute-retarded bombs just miss three Ki-46-11 during an Allied attack on a Japanese airstrip in the South-west Pacific.

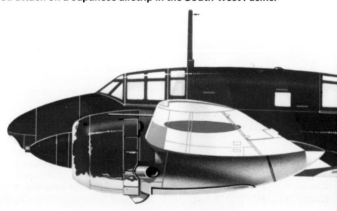

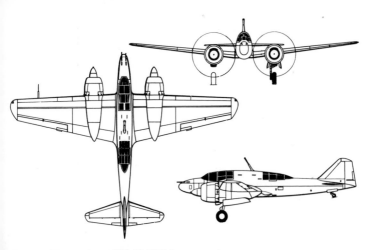

Above: Three-view of Ki-46-III-Kai.

Above: A Ki-46-11 of the 18th Independent Reconnaissance Chutai (Dokuritsu Dai Shijugo Chutai).

Ki-46-III. These entered service in 1943, in which year many earlier versions were converted to Ki-46-II-Kai dual conversion trainers. Total production amounted to 1,742, all made by Mitsubishi at Nagoya and Toyama. Only four prototypes were finished of the turbocharged IVa, but many III models were hastily converted by the Army Tachikawa base into III-Kai night-fighters capable of intercepting B-29s. No radar was carried. At VJ-day Mitsubishi was trying to produce IIIc and IVb fighters and the IIIb ground-attack version.

Above: A Ki-46-III Kai of the 16th Dokuritsu Hikotai. Most of the
Ki-46-IIIs (in all 609 production aircraft were built of this model) were
unarmed reconnaissance machines with a distinctive streamlined shape
without a stepped windscreen. From this was derived the III Kai, also
called Army Type 100 Air Defence Fighter, with conventional windscreen
and a new nose housing two 20mm Ho-5 cannon; the upper mid-
fuselage fuel tank was removed and replaced by a 37mm Ho-203
cannon firing obliquely upward.

Nakajima B5N "Kate"

B5N1 and B5N2

Origin: Nakajima Hikoki KK; also built by Aichi Tokei Denki and Dai-Juichi Kaigun Kokusho (Hiro).
Type: (B5N1) three-seat carrier-based bomber; (2) torpedo bomber.
Engine: (B5N1 Model 11) one 770hp Nakajima Hikari 3 nine-cylinder radial; (B5N1 Model 12) 970 or 985hp Nakajima Sakae 11 14-cylinder two-row radial; (B5N2) 1,115hp Sakae 21.
Dimensions: Span 50ft 11in (15·52m); length (1) 33ft 11in; (2) 33ft 9½in (10·3m); height 12ft 1¾in (3·70m).
Weights: Empty (1) 4,645lb (2107kg); (2) 5,024lb (2279kg); normal loaded (1) 8,047lb (3650kg); (2) 8,378lb (3800kg); maximum loaded (2) 9,039lb (4100kg).
Performance: Maximum speed (1) 217mph (350km/h); (2) 235mph (378km/h); initial climb (both) 1,378ft (420m)/min; service ceiling (both) about 25,000ft (7640m); range (1) 683 miles (1100km); (2) normal gross, 609 miles (980km), overload (4100kg) 1,237 miles (1990km).
Armament: (1) one 7·7mm Type 89 manually aimed from rear cockpit; underwing racks for two 551lb (250kg) or six 132lb (60kg) bombs; (2) two 7·7mm manually aimed from rear cockpit; two 7·7mm fixed above forward fuselage; centreline rack for 1,764lb (800kg, 18in) torpedo or three 551lb bombs.
History: First flight January 1937; (production B5N1) later 1937; (B5N2) December 1939; final delivery, probably 1942.
User: Japan (Imperial Navy).

Development: Designed to meet a 1935 requirement, the B5N was

Below: Probably taken long before Pearl Harbor, this photograph shows early B5N1 attack aircraft, outstanding in their day.

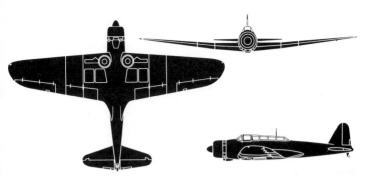

Above: Three-view of B5N1 Model 11.

judged ordinary and obsolescent in World War II, yet in its day it was
advanced and bold. The Japanese keenly studied the stressed-skin aircraft
of Northrop, Douglas and Clark, and swiftly copied new features. The B5N
had not only a thoroughly modern structure but also variable-pitch propeller
(not on RAF Hurricanes until mid-1940!), hydraulically retracting landing
gear, Fowler flaps, NACA cowling, integral wing fuel tanks and, until
judged troublesome, hydraulic wing-folding. The challenging specification
demanded a speed of 330km/h (205mph), but the prototype beat this by
23mph. The B5N1 went into production in time to serve in the Sino-
Japanese war; a few of the rival fixed-gear Mitsubishi B5M were bought as
an insurance. By 1940 some attack B5N were converted into B5N1-K
trainers, but 103 bombed at Pearl Harbor. In the same attack 40 of the new
B5N2 torpedo bombers took part, at least half finding their mark. Subsequently the B5N2 played the chief role in sinking the US carriers *Yorktown*,
Lexington, Wasp and *Hornet*. They soldiered on into 1944 alongside their
replacement the B6N. Total production was 1,149, including 200 by
Aichi and 280 by Hiro Arsenal. Their Allied name was "Kate".

Nakajima B6N Tenzan "Jill"

B6N1, B6N2

Origin: Nakajima Hikoki KK.

Type: Three-seat carrier-based torpedo bomber.

Engine: (B6N1) one 1,870hp Nakajima Mamori 11 14-cylinder two-row radial; (B6N2) 1,850hp Mitsubishi Kasei 25 of same layout.

Dimensions: Span 48ft 10¼in (14·894m); length 35ft 7½in (10·865m); height (1) 12ft 1¾in (3·7m); (2) 12ft 5½in (3·8m).

Weights: Empty 6,636lb (3010kg) (1, 2 almost identical); normal loaded 11,464lb (5200kg); maximum overload 12,456lb (5650kg).

Performance: Maximum speed (1) 289mph (465km/h); (2) 299mph (482km/h); initial climb (1) 1,720ft (525m)/min; (2) 1,885ft (575m)/min; service ceiling (1) 28,379ft (8650m); (2) 29,659ft (9040m); range (normal weight) (1) 907 miles (1460km); (2) 1,084 miles (1745km), (overload) (1) 2,312 miles (3720km); (2) 1,895 miles (3050km).

Armament: One 7·7mm Type 89 manually aimed from rear cockpit and one manually aimed by middle crew-member from rear ventral position, with fixed 7·7mm firing forward in left wing (often absent from B6N1); 1,764lb (800kg, 18in) torpedo carried offset to right of centreline, or six 220lb (100kg) bombs under fuselage.

History: First flight March 1942; service delivery (B6N1) early 1943; (B6N2) December 1943.

User: Japan (Imperial Navy).

Development: Named Tenzan (Heavenly Mountain) after a worshipped mountain in China, and code-named "Jill" by the Allies, the B6N was another conventional-looking aircraft which in fact was in many respects superior to the seemingly more advanced machines of the Allies (in this case the Grumman TBF and Fairey Barracuda). Designed as a replacement

Right: A dramatic photograph, of high quality, showing a B6N2 on fire after being hit by AA fire from USS *Yorktown* near Truk, in the Caroline Islands, on 29 April 1944. Torpedo still in place.

Below: A formation of B6N2s without torpedoes. They are probably painted dark green and pale grey, with black engine cowls. Note the stack of four exhaust pipes behind the engine.

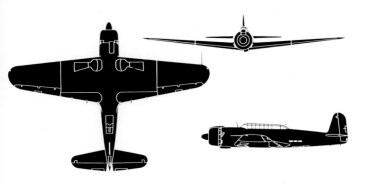

Above: Three-view of B6N2, without radar.

for B5N, Tenzan was slim and clean, with no internal weapon bay. The torpedo was offset, and to increase clearance on torpedo release the big oil cooler was offset in the other direction (to the left). The distinctive shape of the vertical tail was to minimise stowage length in the three-point attitude in carriers. Nakajima's big Mamori engine, driving a four-blade Hamilton-type propeller, suffered severe vibration and overheating, and though the B6N1 was kept in service it was replaced in production by the B6N2. The lower power of the proven Kasei was counteracted by the improved installation with less drag, and jet-thrust from the exhaust stubs. Tenzans went into action off Bougainville in the Marshalls campaign in June 1944. Subsequently they were heavily committed, many being later equipped with ASV radar for night attacks and ending in April-June 1945 with a hectic campaign of torpedo and suicide attacks off Okinawa and Kyushu. By this time the Imperial Navy had no operating carrier and hardly any skilled pilots.

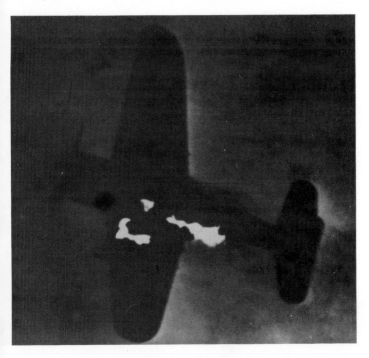

Nakajima J1N1 "Irving"

J1N1-C, J1N1-F, J1N1-S Gekko and J1N1-C-Kai

Origin: Nakajima Hikoki KK.
Type: (C, F) three-seat reconnaissance; (S, C-Kai) two-seat night fighter.
Engines: All operational versions, two 1,130hp Nakajima Sakae 21 14-cylinder two-row radials.
Dimensions: Span 55ft 8½in (16·98m); length (all, excluding nose guns or radar) 39ft 11½in (12·18m); height 14ft 11½in (4·562m).
Weights: Empty (C, S) 10,697lb (4852kg); loaded (C) 15,984lb (7250kg); (S) 15,212lb (6900kg); maximum overload (both) 16,594lb (7527kg).
Performance: Maximum speed (C, S) 315mph (507km/h); initial climb (C, S) 1,968ft (600m)/min; service ceiling 30,578ft (9320m); range (C, S, normal gross) 1,585 miles (2550km), (overload) 2,330 miles (3750km).
Armament: (J1N1-C) one 20mm Type 99 cannon and two 7·7mm Type 97 fixed in nose; (J1N1-S) four 20mm Type 99 Model 2 cannon fixed in rear cockpit, two firing obliquely upwards and two firing obliquely downwards; (J1N1-F) manual dorsal turret with single 20mm gun.
History: First flight May 1941; (production C) August 1942; service delivery (C) end of 1942; first flight (S) August 1943.
User: Japan (Imperial Navy).

Development: In 1938, before the Zero-Sen had flown, the Imperial Navy issued a specification for a twin-engined, long-range escort fighter, to reach a speed of 280 knots, and have a range of 1,300 nautical miles or 2,000 n.m. with extra fuel (the n.m. was the standard naval unit in Japan). Mitsubishi abandoned this project, but Nakajima's design team under K. Nakamura succeeded in producing a large prototype which proved to have remarkable manoeuvrability. Fitted with large fabric-covered ailerons, slotted flaps (opened 15° for combat) and leading-edge slats, it could dog-fight well with a Zero and the prototype was eventually developed to have

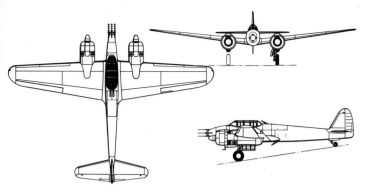

Above: Three-view of J1N1-S Gekko night fighter.

no flight limitations. But the Navy doubted the practicability of the complex scheme of two dorsal barbettes, each mounting two 7·7mm guns, remotely aimed in unison by the navigator. Eventually the Navy decided to buy the J1N1-C with these barbettes removed to serve as a three-seat photographic aircraft. (Some reports claim the failure as a fighter was due to lateral control problems, but Nakajima test pilots insist it was simply a matter of armament.) Soon after sorties began over the Solomons in the spring of 1943 the commander of the 251st Air Corps, Yasuna Kozono, hit on a way of intercepting Allied heavy night bombers. He had several aircraft modified as C-Kai night fighters with upper and lower pairs of oblique cannon. The armament proved effective, and most of the 477 J1N aircraft were built as J1N1-S Gekko (Moonlight) fighters with nose radar and a smoother cabin outline. They were good, robust aircraft, but unable to intercept the fast, high-flying B-29. Their Allied name was "Irving".

Below: The first prototype of the J1N1-C, the production version of the original reconnaissance aircraft.

Nakajima Ki-27 "Nate"
Ki-27a and -27b

Origin: Nakajima Hikoki KK; also built by Mansyu Hikoki Seizo KK.
Type: Single-seat interceptor fighter and light attack.
Engine: Prototype, one 650hp Nakajima Ha-1a (Jupiter-derived) nine-cylinder radial; 27a and 27b, one 710hp Ha-1b.
Dimensions: Span 37ft 0¾in (11·3m); length 24ft 8½in (7·53m); height 9ft 2¼in (2·8m).
Weights: Empty 2,403lb (1090kg); loaded 3,638lb (1650kg); (27b) up to 3,946lb.
Performance: Maximum speed 286mph (460km/h); initial climb 2,953ft (900m)/min; service ceiling, not recorded but about 34,400ft (10,500m); range 389 miles (625km).
Armament: Two 7·7mm Type 89 machine guns fixed in sides of fuselage, firing inside cowling; external racks for four 55lb (25kg) bombs.
History: First flight 15 October 1936; service delivery, early 1938; service delivery (Ki-27b) March 1939; final delivery July 1940.
User: Japan (Imperial Army) and Manchukuo.

Development: The Imperial Japanese Army's first low-wing monoplane fighter, the Ki-27 was in continuous production from 1937 to 1940 and was not only built in much larger quantities than other Japanese aircraft of its day but outnumbered almost every Japanese warplane of World War II. It was designed to meet a 1935 fighter requirement and competed against designs from Kawasaki and Mitsubishi. Though not the fastest, it was easily the most manoeuvrable; in fact it was probably the most manoeuvrable military aircraft of its day and possibly in all history, with plenty of engine power and (the Army having chosen the biggest of three possible sizes of wing) the extremely low loading of 17·9lb/ft². The loaded weight was roughly half that of contemporary Western fighters, and the penalty was paid in light construction and light armament. At the time Japanese pilots cared nothing for speed, fire-power or armour, but sacrificed everything for good visibility and manoeuvrability, and they resisted the introduction of later aircraft such as the Ki-43. Hundreds of Ki-27s fought Chinese and Soviet aircraft over Asia, scoring about 90 per cent of the claimed 1,252 Soviet aircraft (an exaggerated figure) shot down in 1939 after the Nomonhan Incident. Other Ki-27s served with the Manchurian air force, and at the time of Pearl Harbor they outnumbered all other Japanese fighters. Called "Nate" by the Allies, they continued in front-line use throughout the first year of the Pacific War. No fewer than 3,399 were built, 1,379 by the Manchurian (Mansyu Hikoki) company.

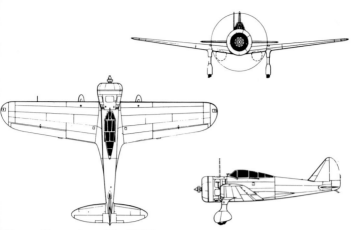

Above: Three-view of the Ki-27b.

Above: The Nakajima Ki-27 appears to have been among the most manoeuvrable fighters of all time, though this quality was gained at the usual expense of light construction and light firepower. These Ki-27b fighters bear the badge of the Akeno fighter training school; most Army pilots in World War II trained on the Ki-27.

Left: This colourful Ki-27b served with the 1st Chutai of the 1st Hikosentai, numerically the pre-eminent flying unit of the Imperial Japanese Army. At the start of World War II this unit was still equipped with this nimble fighter, forming part of the 3rd Hikoshidan for operations against Malaya. In 1942 the Ki-27 was generally replaced by the same builder's Ki-43.

Nakajima Ki-43 Hayabusa "Oscar"

Ki-43-I to Ic, IIa and b, IIIa and b

Origin: Nakajima Hikoki KK; also built by Tachikawa Hikoki KK and Tachikawa Dai-Ichi Rikugun (Arsenal).

Type: Single-seat interceptor fighter (from IIa, fighter-bomber).

Engine: (Ki-43-I series) one 975hp Nakajima Ha-25 (Ha-35/12) Sakae 14-cylinder two-row radial; (II) 1,105hp Ha-115 Sakae; (III) 1,250hp Ha-112 (Ha-33/42) Kasei of same layout.

Dimensions: Span (I) 37ft 10½in; (IIa) 37ft 6¼in (11·437m); (IIb and subsequent) 35ft 6¾in (10·83m); length (I) 28ft 11¾in (8·82m); (II, III) 29ft 3¼in (8·92m); height (all) 10ft 8¾in (3·273m).

Weights: empty (I) 4,354lb (1975kg); normal loaded (I) 5,824lb (2642kg); (II series) 5,825–5,874lb (typically 2655kg); (III) 6,283lb (2850kg).

Performance: Maximum speed (I) 308mph; (II) 320mph (515km/h); (III) 363mph (585km/h); initial climb (typical II) 3,250ft (990m)/min; service ceiling (I) 38,500ft; (II, III) 36,800ft (11,215m); range (I) 746 miles (1200km); (II, III) internal fuel 1,060 miles (1700km), with two 45-gal drop tanks 1,864 miles (3000km).

Armament: (Ia) two 7·7mm Type 80 above engine; (Ib) one 12·7mm, one 7·7mm; (Ic) two 12·7mm; (all II series) two 12·7mm, each with 250 rounds, and wing racks for two 551lb (250kg) bombs; (IIIa) same; (IIIb) two 20mm Ho-5 cannon replacing 12·7mm in top decking, same bomb racks.

History: First flight January 1939; (production Ki-43-I) March 1941; (prototype IIa) February 1942; (prototype IIb) June 1942; (IIIa) December 1944.

Users: Japan (Imperial Army), Thailand; post-war, France (Indo-China) and Indonesia (against Dutch administration).

Development: Code-named "Oscar" by the Allies, the Ki-43 Hayabusa (Peregrine Falcon) was the most numerous of all Imperial Army warplanes and second only in numbers to the Zero-Sen. Compared with the famed Navy fighter it was smaller, lighter and much cheaper to produce. It was cast in the traditional Army mould in which everything was sacrificed for manoeuvrability, though the first prototype (designed by Hideo Itokawa to meet a 1938 Army contract which was simply awarded to Nakajima, without any industrial competition) was very heavy on the controls and disappointing. One prototype was even given fixed landing gear to save weight, but after many changes, and especially after adding a "combat manoeuvre flap" under the wings, the Ki-43 was turned into a dogfighter that could out-manoeuvre every aircraft ever ranged against it. After a few had carelessly got in the way of Allied fighters the more powerful II appeared with some

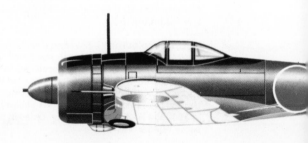

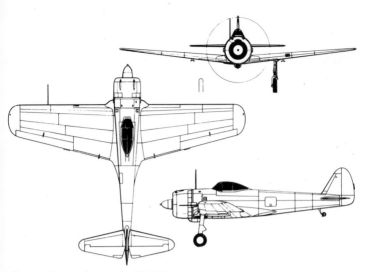

Above: Three-view of the Ki-43-IIa.

armour, self-sealing tanks and slightly reduced span. The mass-produced clipped-wing IIb followed, serving in every Japanese battle. To the end, this nimble fighter remained totally deficient in firepower (except for the few examples of the IIIb at the end of the war), and owing to its very light structure often disintegrated when hit by 0·5in fire. On the other hand, most of Japan's Army aces gained nearly all their scores on this popular little fighter. It was kept in production long after it was obsolete, 5,919 being delivered, including 2,629 by Tachikawa and 49 by the 1st Arsenal.

Above: A puzzling photograph showing what appears to be a Ki-43-Ib being either washed down or (unlikely) refuelled from a bucket. The fighter in the background is a Ki-44 on a trestle with work being done under the tail. Hundreds of Japanese combat aircraft were captured in 1945 but today survivors are pathetically few. There are only three reasonably complete Ki-43s and no Ki-44, and like many surviving World War II aircraft they are not quite authentic, having modern parts added.

Nakajima Ki-44 Shoki "Tojo"

Ki-44-Ia, b and c, IIa, b and c and III

Origin: Nakajima Hikoki KK.

Type: Single-seat interceptor fighter and (II onwards) fighter-bomber.

Engine: (Ia) one 1,260hp Nakajima Ha-41 14-cylinder two-row radial; (Ib and all subsequent) 1,520hp Nakajima Ha-109 of same layout.

Dimensions: Span 31ft (9·448m); length 28ft 8½in (8·75m); height 10ft 8in (3·248m).

Weights: Empty (Ia) 3,968lb (1800kg); (II, typical) 4,643lb (2106kg); normal loaded (no overload permitted) (Ia) 5,622lb (2550kg); (IIc) 6,107lb (2770kg); (III) 5,357lb (2430kg).

Performance: Maximum speed (Ia) 360mph (579km/h); (IIc) 376mph (605km/h); initial climb (IIc) 3,940ft (1200m)/min; service ceiling (IIc) 36,745ft (11,200m); range on internal fuel (typical) 560 miles (900km) (endurance, 2hr 20min).

Armament: (Ia) two 12·7mm Type I in wings and two 7·7mm Type 89 in fuselage; (Ib, IIa, IIb) four 12·7mm Type I, two in fuselage and two in wings, with (II series) wing racks for two 220lb (100kg) bombs; (IIc) two 12·7mm in fuselage, two 40mm Ho-301 low-velocity cannon; (III) two 12·7mm in fuselage, two 20mm Ho-5 cannon in wings.

History: First flight (first of ten prototypes) August 1940; (production Ki-44-Ia) May 1942; (Ib, Ic) 1943; (IIb) December 1943.

User: Japan (Imperial Army).

Development: Marking a complete break with the traditional emphasis on manoeuvrability, the Ki-44 (code-named "Tojo" by the Allies) contrasted with the Ki-43 as did the J2M with the Zero-Sen. Suddenly the need was for greater speed and climb, even at the expense of poorer manoeuvrability and faster landing. In late 1940 a Ki-44 was tested against a Kawasaki Ki-60 and an imported Bf 109E, outflying both; but production was delayed until mid-1942 by the priority accorded the old Ki-43. Pilots did not like the speedy small-winged fighter, with poor view on take-off and such poor control that flick rolls and many other manoeuvres were

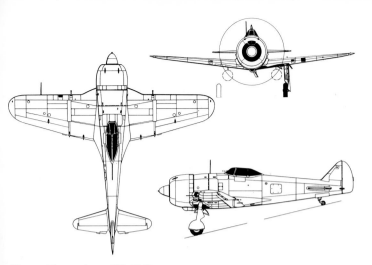

Above: Three-view of Ki-44-IIb.

banned. But gradually the fact that the Ki-44 could climb and dive as well as its enemies brought some measure of popularity, even though many inexperienced pilots were killed in accidents. Most Shokis (Demons) were -II series with retractable tailwheel and other changes, including a glazed teardrop canopy. The heavy cannon of the -IIc, firing caseless ammunition at 400 rounds per minute, were effective against Allied bombers. Probably the most successful mission ever flown in defending Japan was that of 19 February 1945 when a small force of Ki-44 (probably -IIc) climbed up to 120 B-29s and destroyed ten, two reportedly by suicide collisions. Total production was 1,233, including a few of the lightened -III series.

Below: A rare sub-type, the Ki-44-Ic, probably delivered about a year after Pearl Harbor. This model was basically a Ib with wheel-well doors repositioned on the fuselage instead of the legs.

Nakajima Ki-84
Hayate "Frank"

Ki-84-I to Ic, and many projects

Origin: Nakajima Hikoki KK; also built by Mansyu Hikoki Seizo KK and (three Ki-106) Tachikawa Hikoki KK.
Type: Single-seat fighter-bomber.
Engine: In all production models, one 1,900hp Nakajima Homare Ha-45 Model 11 18-cylinder two-row radial.
Dimensions: Span 36ft 10½in (11·238m); length 32ft 6½in (9·92m); height 11ft 1¼in (3·385m).
Weights: Empty 5,864lb (2680kg); normal loaded 8,267lb (3750kg); maximum overload (seldom authorised) 9,150lb (4150kg).
Performance: Maximum speed 388mph (624km/h); initial climb 3,600ft (1100m)/min; service ceiling 34,450ft (10,500m); range on internal fuel 1,025 miles (1650km); range with 98-gal drop tanks, 1,815 miles (2920km).
Armament: (Ia) two 20mm Ho-5 in wings, each with 150 rounds, and two 12·7mm Type 103 in top of fuselage with 350 rounds; (Ib) four 20mm, each with 150 rounds, two in wings and two in fuselage; (Ic) two 20mm in fuselage and two 30mm Ho-105 cannon in wings; (all operational models) two racks under outer wings for tanks or bombs up to 551lb (250kg) each.
History: First flight March 1943; (production Ia) August 1943; service delivery April 1944.
User: Japan (Imperial Army).

Development: Code-named "Frank" by the Allies, the Ki-84 of the Imperial Army was generally regarded as the best Japanese fighter of World War II. Yet it was not without its problems. Part of its fine all-round performance stemmed from the extremely advanced direct-injection engine, the first Army version of the Navy NK9A; yet this engine gave constant trouble and needed skilled maintenance. T. Koyama designed the Ki-84 to greater strength factors than any earlier Japanese warplane, yet poor heat-treatment of the high-strength steel meant that landing gears often simply snapped. Progressive deterioration in quality control meant that pilots never knew how particular aircraft would perform, whether the brakes would work or whether, in trying to intercept B-29s over Japan, they would even ▶

Above: Most Japanese fighters were camouflaged in overall dark green (as at right) or in mottled shades, but this attractive Ki-84-Ia painted pale grey served with HQ Chutai, 29th Sentai, on Taiwan (Formosa) in the summer of 1945.

Right: Another Ki-84-Ia series, this Hayate was on the strength of the 58th Shimbu-Tai in the home defence of Japan at the end of the war.

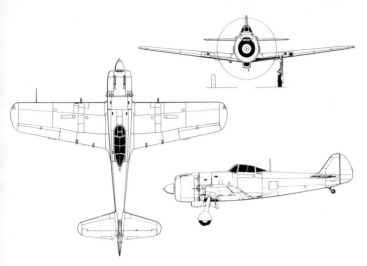

Above: Three-view of Ki-84-la.

Above: A shotai (section of three aircraft) from the
52nd Sentai photographed in late 1944 when about to
leave on a long-range attack mission. Each carries one
drop tank and one bomb, a tricky combination which
inevitably means lateral-control problems as fuel is
consumed. The usual size of bomb was 250kg (551lb).

Above: Another Ki-84-la serving in the southwest Pacific in 1944, in this case with the 11th Sentai. A detail visible in this picture is that the 'butterfly' combat flaps are lowered.

be able to climb high enough. Despite this, the Ki-84 was potentially superb, a captured -la out-climbing and outmanoeuvring a P-51H and P-47N! First batches went to China, where the 22nd Sentai flew rings round Gen Chennault's 14th Air Force. The unit then moved to the Philippines, where the rot set in, with accidents, shortages and extremely poor serviceability. Frequent bombing of the Musashi engine factory and extreme need to conserve raw material led to various projects and prototypes made of wood (Ki-84-II series and Ki-106) or steel (Ki-113) and advanced models with the 2,000hp Ha-45ru turbo charged engine, Ha-45/44 with two-stage three-speed blower and 2,500hp Ha-44/13. Total production of the Hayate (Hurricane) was 3,514 (2,689 at Ohta, 727 at Utsonomiya and 95 in Manchuria by Mansyu, which also flew the Ki-116 with smaller Ha-112 engine) and three at Tachikawa.

Above and right: Two more attractively painted Ki-84-la fighters which saw action in the Pacific campaigns. Above, with the 1st Chutai, 47th Sentai, based at Narumatsu; right, with the 1st Chutai, 73rd Senai, Philippines, December 1944. Combat victories were not painted on aircraft.

Above: An early Ki-84-Ia Hayate. The long landing gears were prone to structural failure, as a result of faulty heat-treatment of the steel legs, and the complex and closely cowled engine gave prolonged trouble; so did the hydraulics.

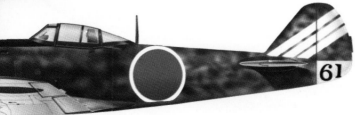

Yokosuka D4Y Suisei "Judy"
D4Y1 and 1-C, D4Y2, 2-C and 2-S, D4Y3 and D4Y4

Origin: Dai-Ichi Kaigun Koku Gijitsusho, Yokosuka; production aircraft built by Aichi Kokuki KK and Dai-Juichi Kaigun Kokusho.

Type: Two-seat carrier dive bomber; (1-C, 2-C, reconnaissance; 2-S night fighter; D4Y4, single-seat Kamikaze).

Engines: (1) one 1,200hp Aichi Atsuta 21 inverted-vee-12 liquid-cooled (Daimler-Benz 601); (2) 1,400hp Atsuta 32; (3, 4) 1,560hp Mitsubishi Kinsei 62 14-cylinder two-row radial).

Dimensions: Span (1, 2) 37ft 8½in (11·493m); (3, 4) 37ft 9in (11·50m); length (all, despite engine change) 33ft 6½in (10·22m); height (1, 2) 12ft 1in (3·67m); (3, 4) 12ft 3¼in (3·74m).

Weights: Empty (1) 5,650lb (2565kg); (2) 5,840lb (2635kg); (3) 5,512lb (2501kg); (4) variable; maximum loaded (1) 9,615lb (4361kg); (2) 9,957lb (4353kg); (3) 10,267lb (4657kg); (4) 10,434lb (4733kg).

Performance: Maximum speed (1) 339mph (546km/h); (2) 360mph (580km/h); (3) 356mph (574km/h); initial climb (1) 1,970ft (600m)/min; (others) 2,700ft (820m)/min; service ceiling (typical) 34,500ft (10,500m); range (2) 749 miles (1205km); (3) 945 miles (1520km).

Armament: Normally, two 7·7mm Type 97 fixed above engine, one 7·7mm manually aimed from rear cockpit; internal bomb bay for single 551lb (250kg) bomb, plus one 66lb (30kg) bomb under each wing; (4) see text.

History: First flight November 1940; (production D4Y1) May 1941; service delivery, late' 1941.

User: Japan (Imperial Navy).

Development: Designed to a challenging specification of the Imperial Japanese Navy of 1937, which called for a long-range two-seat dive bomber as fast as the "Zero" fighter, the D4Y was one of the very few Japanese aircraft to go into production with a liquid-cooled engine. The supposed lower drag of such an engine had been one of the factors in meeting the requirement, but the Japanese version of the DB 601 had an unhappy history in carrier service. The first D4Y versions in combat were 1-C reconnaissance aircraft flying from the carrier *Soryu* during the Battle

Below: A D4Y3 Suisei Model 33, with two 72.6 Imp gal drop tanks. By the time this radial-engined model was delivered nearly all Suiseis had to be assigned to land-based units.

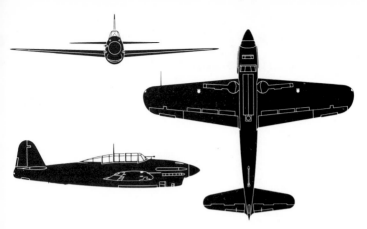

Above: Three-view of D4Y1 (D4Y2 very similar).

of Midway in June 1942. The carrier was sunk in that encounter, and soon most D4Y were being operated by unskilled crews from island airstrips. In 1943 the main problems with the aircraft — named Suisei (Comet), and called "Judy" by the Allies — were solved by switching to the smooth and reliable radial engine. During the final year of the war the D4Y4 appeared as a single-seat suicide attacker carrying 1,764lb (800kg) of explosives, while some dozens of Atsuta-engined examples were turned into 2-S night fighters with one or two 20mm cannon fixed obliquely behind the rear cockpit. Total production was 2,038.

Below: The US Navy identified this suicide attacker as a D4Y4, the specially converted single-seat D4Y version (though it seems to have fixed landing gears). It hit the cruiser *Columbia* at Lingayen Gulf on 6 January 1945, causing much damage.

Yokosuka MXY-7 Ohka "Baka

MXY-7 Model 11 and Model 22

Origin: Dai-Ichi Kaigun Koku Gijitsusho, Yokosuka; 600 Model 11 built by Dai-Ichi Kaigun Kokusho.

Type: Single-seat piloted missile for surface attack.

Engine: (11) one three-barrel Type 4 Model 20 rocket motor with sea-level thrust of 1,764lb (800kg); (22) TSU-11 jet engine, with piston-engined compressor, rated at 441lb (200kg) thrust.

Dimensions: Span (11) 16ft 4¾in (5m); (22) 13ft 6¼in (4·12m); length (11) 19ft 10¾in (6·07m); (22) 22ft 6¾in (6·88m); height (both) about 3ft 11¼in (1·20m).

Weights: Empty (no warhead) (11) 970lb (440kg); (22) 1,202lb (545kg); loaded (11) 4,718lb (2140kg); (22) 3,200lb (1450kg).

Performance: Maximum speed on level (11) 534mph (860km/h); (22) about 300mph (480km/h); final dive speed (both) 621mph (1000km/h); climb and ceiling, normally launched at about 27,000ft (8200m); range (11) 55 miles (88km).

Armament: (11) warhead containing 2,645lb (1200kg) of tri-nitroaminol; (22) warhead weight 1,323lb (600kg).

History: Start of design August 1944; start of quantity production (11) September 1944; service delivery, early October 1944.

User: Japan (Imperial Navy).

Development: Having accepted the principle of the Kamikaze suicide attack, the Imperial Navy was only logical in designing an aircraft for this duty instead of using inefficient and more vulnerable conventional machines having less devastating effect. Built partly of wood, Model 11 was carried

Below: a genuine operational Model 11, complete with warhead and motor, found abandoned (probably on Okinawa). All Ohka variants carried a cherry blossom motif on the side of the fuselage (here partly obscured by the joint strap). What appears to be a pitot head above the fuselage is probably not part of the aircraft.

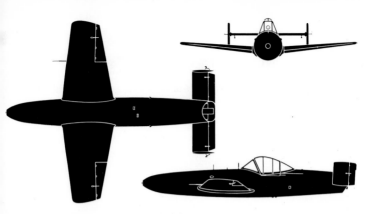

Above: Three-view of MXY-7 Model 11.

aloft by a G4M ("Betty"), without bomb doors and specially modified for the task, and released about 50 miles from the target. The pilot then held a fast glide at about 290mph (466km/h), electrically igniting the rocket while pushing over into a steep final dive for the last 30 seconds of trajectory. Though nearly all these missiles failed to reach their objectives, the few that did wrought fearful havoc. Ohka (Cherry Blossom) was called "Baka" (Japanese for "fool") by the Allies, which was not very appropriate. Several manufacturers delivered 755, and 45 unpowered K-1 versions were delivered for training. The Model 22, of which some 50 were delivered, was underpowered. Not completed by VJ-day, the Model 33 would have had the Ne-20 turbojet; Models 43A and 43B were for launching from submarines and land catapults, respectively, but these too failed to see service.

Below: A fully operational Ohka Model 11 found on Yontan airfield, Okinawa, an island infested with these missiles. The three nozzles of the solid-propellant rocket motor can be seen, as can the serial number 1022 on one rudder and the rear fuselage. The aircraft in the background appears to be an Army Ki-61 fighter.

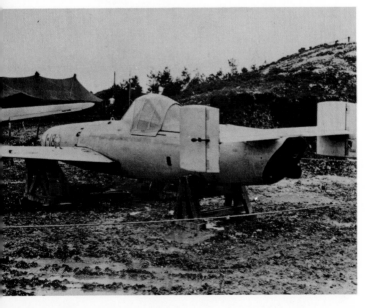

Yokosuka P1Y1 Ginga "Frances

P1Y1 Model 11, P1Y1-S, P1Y2 and 2-S

Origin: Design by Dai-Ichi Kaigun Koku Gijitsusho, but all construction by Nakajima Hikoki KK and Kawanishi Kokuki KK.

Type: Three-seat multi-role attack bomber; -S, two-seat night fighter.

Engines: (1) two 1,820hp Nakajima Ho-21 Homare 11 18-cylinder two-row radials; (2) 1,825hp Mitsubishi Kasei 25 14-cylinder two-row radials.

Dimensions: Span 65ft 7½in (20m); length 49ft 2½in (15m); height 14ft 1¼in (4·30m)

Weights: Empty (1) 14,748lb (6690kg); normal loaded (1) 23,148lb (10,500kg); maximum loaded (1) 29,762lb (13,500kg).

Performance: Maximum speed (1) 345mph (556km/h); (2) 354mph (570km/h); initial climb (1) 2,100ft (650m)/min; service ceiling 33,530ft (10,220m); range (1) 2,728 miles (4390km).

Armament: (1 and 2) one 20mm Type 99-II cannon manually aimed from nose, one 20mm or 12·7mm manually aimed from rear cockpit (a few aircraft had dorsal turret with two 20mm or 12·7mm); internal bay for two 551lb (250kg) bombs, plus small bombs beneath outer wings; as alternative, one 1,764lb (800kg) or 1,874lb (850kg) torpedo externally, or two 1,102lb (500kg) bombs inboard of engines; (1-S, 2-S) two 20mm fixed firing obliquely upward in centre fuselage, plus single 20mm aimed from rear cockpit, or powered dorsal turret with two 20mm.

History: First flight (Y-20 prototype) early 1943; (production P1Y1) August 1943; (prototype P1Y2-S) June 1944.

User: Japan (Imperial Navy).

Development: Similar to late-model Ju 88 aircraft in size, power and

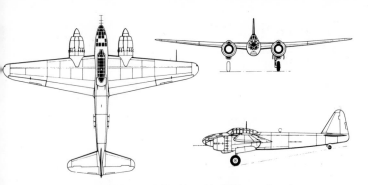

Above: Three-view of late-model P1Y1 with ASV search radar.

capability, this fine-looking aircraft was one of the best designed in Japan during World War II. The 1940 Navy specification called for a land-based aircraft capable of level and dive bombing, but by the time production began at the Nakajima factories at Koizumi and Fukushima it had already become a torpedo bomber, and it was to do much more before its brief career was over. At sea level it could outrun many Allied fighters and it was manoeuvrable and well protected; yet it carried 1,290gal of fuel and had greater range than any other aircraft in its class. Called Ginga (Milky Way), and christened "Frances" by the Allies, this machine would have been a menace had it not been crippled by lack of skilled crews, lack of fuel and lack of spares. Nevertheless Nakajima built 1,002, of which some were used as suicide aircraft while a few were converted into the P1Y1-S night fighter. Kawanishi had meanwhile developed a completely new version, the Kasei-engined P1Y2, and delivered 96 P1Y2-S night fighters called Kyokko (Aurora), which saw little action.

Left: This appears to be one of the unpainted P1Y1 development prototypes; it almost certainly has a retractable tailwheel, a sure means of identifying pre-production machines, and subsequent aircraft were invariably fully painted. An outstanding aircraft in almost all respects, the P1Y1 was used for numerous trials and research programmes including tests of radars, weapons and the first small Japanese turbojet. One model was to have been armed with 16 forward-firing 20mm cannon.

Below: A dramatic photograph showing a P1Y1 making a suicide attack on an American warship (whose AA fire is visible) while pursued by an F4U Corsair which has hit the left engine.

OTHER GUIDES IN THIS SERIES....

AN ILLUSTRATED GUIDE TO

MODERN
FIGHTERS
AND ATTACK AIRCRAFT

Fact-packed
descriptions of
60 of the world's
most exciting
warplanes

120 action photographs
most in full colour
180 line drawings
34 superb
colour profiles

Bill Gunston

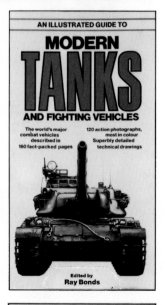

AN ILLUSTRATED GUIDE TO

MODERN
TANKS
AND FIGHTING VEHICLES

The world's major
combat vehicles
described in
160 fact-packed pages

120 action photographs,
most in colour
Superbly detailed
technical drawings

Edited by
Ray Bonds

AN ILLUSTRATED GUIDE TO

MODERN
WARSHIPS
Over 60 of the world's most exciting warships

160 fact-packed
pages in colour

130 action photographs
Over 60 technical
drawings

Hugh Lyon

AN ILLUSTRATED GUIDE TO

BOMBERS
OF WORLD WAR II

160 fact-packed
pages in colour
Descriptions of well over
50 aircraft types,
plus many variants

More than 140
detailed line drawings
90 dramatic photographs,
many in colour
Over 40 colour drawings

Bill Gunston

* Each has 160 fact-filled pages
* Each is colourfully illustrated with hundreds of action photographs and technical drawings
* Each contains concisely presented data and accurate descriptions of major international weapons
* Each represents tremendous value

Further titles in this series are in preparation
Your military library will be incomplete without them.

PRINTED IN BELGIUM BY

INTERNATIONAL BOOK PRODUCTION